TRUSTED

TRUSTED

THE PROVEN PATH TO CUSTOMER
LOYALTY AND BUSINESS GROWTH

By

Natalie Doyle Oldfield

Trusted. The Proven Path to Customer Loyalty and Business Growth

Copyright © 2024 by Natalie C. Doyle Oldfield

This publication is designed to provide accurate and authoritative information regarding the subject matter covered. It is sold with the understanding that the author is not engaged in rendering legal, accounting, health or other professional advice. Any perceived slight of any individual or organization is purely unintentional.

Library and archives Canada data

Title: Trusted The Proven Path to Customer Loyalty and Business Growth

Names: Oldfield, Natalie Doyle, author

ISBN: 979-8-89316-760-3 - eBook
ISBN: 979-8-89316-778-8 - Paperback
ISBN: 979-8-89316-779-5 - Hardcover

Although the author has made every effort to ensure that the information in this book was correct at press time, the author does not assume and hereby disclaim any liability to any party for any loss, damage, or disruption caused by errors or omissions, whether such errors or omissions result from negligence, accident, or any other cause.

Adherence to all applicable laws and regulations, including international, federal, provincial, state and local governing professional licensing, business practices, advertising, and all other aspects of doing business in Canada or the US, or any other jurisdiction is the sole responsibility of the reader and consumer.

For more information, email NOldfield@SuccessThroughTrust.com

To Michael, Patrick and Courtney

CONTENTS

What I Decided To Find Out and How It Will Change Your Business

Let's start with a question, which might be the most significant business question of all: *Is there a singular factor that can make or break your company, your firm, your business, or your organization?*

My whole career, I've been fascinated with a few simple questions. What makes people tick? Why and how do customers decide to buy? Why do some companies succeed, and others fail?

I was intrigued with these questions, so several years ago, I enrolled in graduate school to seek the answers. Intuitively I knew people do business with people they know, like and trust. I wanted to dive deeper into that.

In September 2009, I began a research project, and the results made my jaw drop.

My research focused on successful companies. I wanted to find out if there was a singular factor that could make or break a company. In my research, I learned that 'trust' is that make-or-break factor I was seeking, especially customer trust. It is the singular factor that can predict an organization's success or failure. It is the most critical asset a company has: the trust of its employees, customers, and partners. Yes, trust is an asset. It can be measured and managed.

Organizations are facing greater scrutiny from a more informed and critical customer than ever before. The tolerance level of disingenuous activity will continue to fall. As a result, customers all over the world are prioritizing purchasing from companies displaying trustworthy behaviour.

Customers are empowered, they are skeptical, they are paying attention, and they are demanding more accountability and transparency. We want to buy from, support and do business with people and organizations we trust.

Your ability to build trust has a profound impact on your results. In fact, without your customer's trust, you will eventually cease to exist as an organization.

The results of my research, which I share in the introduction, inspired me write this book for you. I wrote it for you, the business owner, the manager, and leader, along with those who aspire to that level of accomplishment. I want business owners and leaders like you to be aware, to have the tools, to become THE MOST *Trusted* in your industry. To grow your businesses and to achieve the success and results you work so hard for.

Over several years of study and research I was able to make empirical deductions directly from data gathered in the field. I wanted to build a practical trust model from the ground up, derived from evidence; a methodology and a disciplined approach organizations can apply to achieve results. When I started, the problem was how to measure trust well enough to enable leaders to manage it with their staff, customers, partners and external stakeholders. Knowing what gets measured gets managed, I developed the proprietary Client Trust Index™, which we use to measure trustworthiness, that precious asset I call Trust Equity™.

My earlier book, *The Power of Trust: How Top Companies Build, Manage and Protect It*, (2017) tells the story of how the Building and Protecting Trust Model and the Client Trust Index™ was developed and tested, so that it could be applied in the real world. The Client Trust Index™, measures Trust Equity™ and customer sentiment. It provides a quantifiable score, so that companies can benchmark and use it as a key performance indicator. The data and the insights identify any gaps and suggest opportunities for improvement and growth.

Since developing the Client Trust Index™, the Eight Principles of Trust, the Trust Building, Strengthening and Protecting Model and coining the term Trust Equity™ in 2009, I've used these frameworks, tools, systems and models with individuals and organizations alike and seen both transform for the better. Hundreds of successful owners, CEOs and leaders have been in my consulting programs and training and development sessions and have grown their companies by focusing on growing customer trust. They have reported consistent results from their work on trust: more sales, more repeat business, attracting customers faster, enhanced customer focus, increased employee engagement, increased sales sensitivity, fewer cancelled orders, and more understanding from partners when the inevitable problems arise.

The Power of Trust laid out the theoretical and practical underpinnings of my research, which has been published in a peer-reviewed journal and held to exacting academic standards.

In *Trusted*, you'll meet real people dealing with business issues in their organizations, as I take you through the steps toward understanding how trusted your organization is, what the potential risks are and what practical steps can be taken to protect and enhance trust. This is the book where the research from *The Power of Trust* comes to life in real situations and real businesses.

Trust is not just a concept or idea. It is a measurable and manageable factor that is crucial to the success of every business and every organization. It is an asset that successful companies use to profit from managing that asset well. Trust can be learned, and your organization can master it.

Following the evidence - based methods set out in this book, any company can learn how to cultivate and develop relationships of trust. Trust is a skill set. It can be learned, measured, and improved.

Trusted is the culmination of my work over the last 15 years researching and working with some of the world's most successful companies.

Each chapter begins with a true story and each chapter is a principle of Trust. The names of the people and organizations have been changed to protect client confidentiality, but all events, timelines and results are true. These are real-world examples from real companies where they made it happen, and made it stick. As you read these stories and the principles of trust they teach, you'll be able to reflect on stories in your own organization and see the parallels.

Knowing how to change things in your business to get what you want is a total game changer. Your business is about to change in the most amazing ways. You are not alone on this journey. This book is here to guide you through the proven path.

Are you ready to start?

Here we go. I am excited for you!

Yours truly,
Natalie Doyle Oldfield

"Relationships are the lifeblood of your business. That must be protected."

-Natalie Doyle Oldfield

Warning Signals, Hidden Dangers, Red Flags and Blind Spots

Your company's very efficient and accomplished Chief Technology Officer is asked to speak at one of your industry's most important conferences. The timing, the event and the audience are all perfect. All your major customers will be there.

Last quarter, the company shared with key customers an important change that was coming: the CTO, who we'll call "Chris", will be taking over as the new owner. The president of the past 20 years is easing himself out of the business. The conference presents a perfect opportunity for the industry to meet Chris, the new owner.

Everyone in the company is excited. Chris, who has helped build the company for 20 years is excited. Your company invests, plans, and you exhibit in the conference trade show. You hire a professional to help develop the speech and coach Chris to give a fantastic presentation.

The day of the presentation arrives, and Chris gets up on stage and takes the microphone. Despite the preparation, he appears nervous and uncomfortable. He fumbles with the microphone, looking like he doesn't want to be there. He starts his presentation and immediately sounds over-prepared and over-practiced. He's speaking in a monotone. Somehow, Chris gets through the presentation, and the audience of industry insiders is kind and give him a nice round of applause.

Now, it's time for the live question and answer portion. And this is when the fun-not-fun really started.

Chris' response to the first query is abrupt: "That's not a good question," he tells the questioner, "Here is a better way to look at it," and proceeds to correct the audience member for his folly in asking "the wrong question." The head of marketing had seen glimpses of this attitude in the past in internal meetings. They thought the speech coach would have addressed this.

The second question from the audience is about an issue that is continually coming up in their industry. Chris bluntly tells the second questioner, "That is not our concern, I've been told it affects many in the industry, but not us."

The next question wasn't about the topic of the speech. An audience member asked, "What are your plans for the future of the company?" Given the circumstances with Chris taking over the company, this was understandable and straightforward. But Chris shrugged it off. "This isn't the time or the place," he said, dismissively. "Those that need to know that, do. Next question?"

Little wonder the room had become very quiet. Chris, the CTO and owner, was coming off as arrogant and combative. To be fair, he was not a professional speaker, and many people feel intimidated by speaking in public. But Chris seemed to lack empathy and to be bored with his audience. More importantly, he introduced doubt and uncertainty about himself and the organization.

He undermined trust in his leadership and therefore in the company.

Chris had earned his career success. He is brilliant, hardworking, competent and results oriented. He built many of the company's products and spent years working in the trenches. He cares about the company and is willing to do whatever it takes to help it grow. But Chris was committing a cardinal sin in client relations, with his words and interactions, it was clear that he was thinking more of his own concerns than theirs.

It would be simple to write this off as a lack of presentation skill or ability to answer questions in real time. It would be easy to shrug your shoulders and say, *"Some people have it, some people don't."*

However, in this case, "It" is not the ability to present a speech or answer questions flawlessly, but in this case, "it" is the ability to consistently build relationships of trust, to project confidence and trustworthiness.

When it comes to inherently knowing how to become Trusted, some people have it, and some people don't.

Imagine if everyone – from the customer experience representatives to the C-Suite executives - was Trusted. If every single person in your organization knew how to deliberately build, cultivate, and develop relationships of trust with customers, with colleagues, with stakeholders. How would that skill have changed Chris' presentation and Q&A? How would that support the organization through this time of transition in leadership?

Companies and leaders succeed not because they are smarter, or more agile. They succeed because they know how to build relationships of trust. In a survey 600 business executives across North America, Europe and Asia Pacific, Economist Impact found high levels of trust are beneficial for company's financial success. Trust boosts an organizations market competitiveness, customer loyalty and satisfaction, raises productivity, aids recruitment and retention of talent, and ultimately, secures long term revenue growth.[1] Trustworthy companies outperform non-trustworthy companies by 2.5 times.[2] A PwC study reports 93% of business executives agree the ability to build and maintain trust improves the bottom line. [3] In that same study, PwC reports 61% of consumers have recommended a company that they trust to friends or family, 46% purchased more, and 28% paid a premium.

Becoming Trusted begins with looking in the mirror. It looks like taking the opportunity to ask yourself: How do I really show up? How do others see me? What impression do I make? How self-aware am I? How would colleagues and co-workers rate my trustworthiness? How would customers rate my trustworthiness?

Asking yourself these questions is a great place to start.

When it comes to being a trusted individual, some people have "it" and some don't, yet that can be fixed. Trust is a leadership skill that can be developed and cultivated. This book will show you how.

Heed the Signals of Potential Trouble with Trust

The first warning signs that you have an issue with trust might show up through finding out about a project your customer is working on with another company, on something you could have handled. There might be a lack of response, the feeling of being ghosted, a notification that your customer is 'trying out' a new provider or planning to issue a Request for Proposal for the offerings you currently provide for them. Though these may seem like normal business issues, at their core, they are warning signals you may have a trust issue with customers.

Other business problems that have a lack of trust at their core include:

- Declining revenues
- Fewer sales and lost business
- More complaints
- Leads for new business slipping away
- Lack of repeat business, starting each quarter fresh
- Problems with customer retention

- Longer sales cycles

- Fewer customer referrals

- Fewer partnership opportunities

- Customer skepticism

- Customers questioning your reliability, asking for more details or for another proposal

If your company is experiencing one or more of these warning signals, you most likely have a trust issue. And that can be fixed. Trust is the life blood that runs through your business. Trust is the most important thing to exist in your business, to be developed, to be successful. It runs through all of our relationships. Paying due attention to this root cause of your company's trust factor can change the trajectory of your success.

Even more concerning – the indication that you have a systemic trust issue rarely starts with a formal complaint from customers. 96% of unhappy customers don't complain at all, and 91% of those will simply leave and never come back, according to research completed by 1st Financial Training services.

Trust is established, strengthened, and maintained through the sum of the experiences a customer has with everyone in a company. Yes, *everyone*. Every employee has a part to play in the customer's decision to buy, to invest, to support and to trust you and your company.

Imagine if every single individual who interacts with customers, partners and or external stakeholders knew how to build, manage, and grow relationships of trust? What would that look like? What would that mean for your company? What would that mean for you as an individual?

A global survey conducted by Salesforce Research reported that 86% of business buyers expected a trusted advisor relationship with sales reps, yet 73% of business buyers say most sales interactions feel transactional.[4]

People want to buy from people they have a relationship with and that starts with trust.

What would be the impact on your company if everyone was a master trust builder? If everyone learned how to build trust? If everyone was viewed as a trusted advisor to customers? If everyone was paying attention to the company's critical trust risk points?

As detailed in my book *The Power of Trust: How Top Companies Build, Manage and Protect It,* a **critical trust risk point is anything that might undermine trust or confidence in your business.** In other words, critical trust points are any interactions with a company where trust can be gained or lost.

12 Common Trust Risk Points Many Businesses Face:

1. Inappropriate employee behavior

2. Security, privacy, or data breach issues

3. Responding poorly to customer complaints

4. Failure to meet customer service expectations

5. Product or service deficiencies

6. Customer or employee safety

7. Arguing with customers

8. How you handle returns, warranty, and service issues

9. Failure to admit mistakes

10. Direct conflicts of interest

11. Not listening to the customer

12. Failure to act in the customer's best interests

Identifying Critical Trust Risk Points In Your Business

The one thing these twelve risk points have in common? People.

Your people and how they communicate, how they behave and how they serve are the most critical trust risk point organizations have. Frontline employees have a significant impact on the customer's decision to do business with you and your company. Employees who lack empathy, patience, or knowledge or who are insincere, dishonest, or disengaged, create barriers for customers to do business with you. Any systemic lack of focus on the customer is the most prevalent trust risk point businesses have.

Some business owners and leaders overlook trust risk points until there is an impending threat to the company. Many of the risk points listed above are not always obvious and can be easy to hide: they might include unethical or inappropriate employee behavior, negative attitudes, employee fraud or violating confidentiality understandings.

What are the trust risk points and the moments that matter most to your customer?

One way to discover your critical trust risk points is to think about the customer's experience with your company, from the time they first hear of you, before they really know you, to when they start educating themselves, to the evaluation stage, to the first contact, the sales process, the decision, the purchase, implementation and so on. Every step of the digital and the physical journey with your customer should be considered.

Different companies and different industries have their own unique trust risk points. For example:

In Principle # 1, we'll examine a critical trust risk point and a "moment that matters" to customers of a cyber security firm; when they call in for technical support and how they are treated by the front-facing staff.

In Principle # 7, I share a personal story of receiving a bill from an accountant, that uncovered a lack of respect in their attitude toward myself as the client.

Among manufacturing companies there is risk in losing trust in matters related to product quality, in potential supplier disputes, in delivery problems, price issues, poor service and post-purchase support.

With construction companies trust might be lost around labor disputes and construction delays, missed deadlines, budget overruns or problems with field service technicians' relations with customers.

Professional services firms encounter trust risk points in lack of follow-up, poor advice, unethical employee behavior, disputes over billable hours, conflict of interest and managing client expectations.

Every business is unique. It's important to take the time to think about who, what and where your critical trust points are. Where in the customer journey are there opportunities to gain or lose customer trust? Where are your vulnerabilities? What are you doing about them?

Here's something else to consider – your trust-building abilities don't just affect whether you're able to keep the customers you've worked so hard to win. Trust affects every area of your business, including the money you might already be wasting on sales and marketing. Here's why:

We all prefer to do business with people we know, like and trust. The fact is that **we decide to trust first, then we decide to buy.** That makes trust the biggest barrier and the biggest enabler to your success. It is the reason a customer does or doesn't choose you. Your ability to build trust shines through in everything you do to acquire leads, sell to customers, and deliver what you've sold. But trust shouldn't be a mysterious or elusive concept.

I've created a framework and step-by-step measurable, evidence-based system for you to build trust with customers. You no longer need to throw spaghetti at the wall to try and figure out what is causing a revenue problem, an engagement problem, or a customer communications problem. We can measure the trust your customers have in you and because we can measure it, you can manage it. I've taken hundreds of companies through the Trust Mastery program, where I guide your team to take specific steps to increase trust with customers. And, in this book, we are going to unpack everything I've uncovered in the years of research, consulting, and training, to get to the heart of how we decide to trust.

If you have bought this book, you are ambitious by definition. You want to be the most trusted in your industry and in your market. You know the trust factor is built on the premise that when you take action, things improve in your business. You might have the best products in the world, with the most patents along with talented and committed employees, however you cannot deliver long-term success without loyal customers built through strong relationships founded on trust.

The Science and the Evidence

The Trust Triangle

When asked if you trust a person or a company, chances are you could answer yes or no. However, if I follow up by asking how much you trust them, you may not be so clear. Trust can feel difficult to quantify. When we think of how it works or how to express it, it can feel like a fuzzy concept, something esoteric or ethereal.

Yet intuitively, we already know a lot about trust. It is part of every interaction in our lives. We know very clearly when we don't trust someone. We know how it feels when someone may be hiding something from us, or they're not telling the whole truth. Maybe they are saying one thing but doing another, or serving their own interests and not yours, or their behaviour is unethical. You just don't trust them, or what they're selling.

But sometimes you meet an individual, and the opposite happens, you just inherently trust them. Why is that the case?

Trust is difficult to see, to describe and to quantify. You can't touch it, hear it, or smell it. But it is real. We understand it naturally, intuitively, and our inner alarms go off when it's damaged or absent. Trust is complex, it's complicated and it is time based.

THE TRUST TRIANGLE

Trust has three components that form an integrated model. They include *communication* that is clear, empathetic, consistent, honest, and transparent, *behaviour* that is reliable, ethical, and focused on motives to act in the customer's best interests and *service* that is sincere, predictable, reliable, empathetic, and committed to the long term.

All three components must be present. Like a triangle, all three sides must be in place, each side supporting the other two, all of them vital to their stability and strength.

By the same token, you can't expect to be trusted if you exhibit poor behaviour, regardless of how well you communicate. Behaviour is at the base of the triangle and is the underpinning of the whole structure. It is the foundation of trust.

We decide consciously and subconsciously to trust a company and its employees based on our cumulative interactions and experiences with them. This is especially true about how the organization behaves toward us and how it serves our interests.

This Triangle of Trust Model and The Eight Principles of Trust are the foundation of the Client Trust Index™ which provides factual evidence of customer trust, a Trust Equity™ score and measures true customer sentiment. This evidence-based tool provides a model and a toolkit to help organizations build, strengthen and protect the trust their customers.

The Eight Principles of Trust

We decide to have confidence based on our experiences with companies and how they apply the Eight Principles of Trust that have been identified through our research.

The Eight Principles of Trust can mistakenly be interpreted as eight distinct action items that can be addressed in isolation; however, all eight principles must be present and all work together. They form an interrelated model, and if your organization violates even one of them, it undermines trust. And you have a potentially lethal trust issue in the making.

The Eight Principles of Trust are in fact how customers and stakeholders decide to trust an organization. When an organization or an individual applies the Eight Principles of Trust to how it communicates, behaves, and serves customers, trust will be built.

THE EIGHT PRINCIPLES OF BUILDING, PROTECTING AND STRENGTHENING TRUST

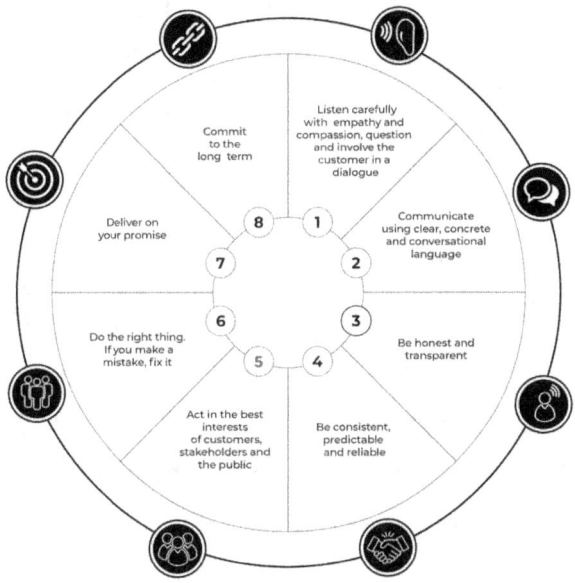

Like a chain with a single broken link, trust deteriorates to the point of unreliability if just one principle is not applied to the relationship, or if one principle is violated.

Trust is Measurable, Quantifiable, and Repeatable

Trust Equity™ is the amount of trust an organization has with its customers or stakeholders. Trust is an organizations most important asset. When a company prioritizes and purposefully builds relationships of trust, the more Trust Equity™ accrues.

A company's Trust Equity™ score is a predictor of future success and loyalty.

My research found a statistically significant, positive correlation between trust and:

- Loyalty
- Commitment
- Likelihood to recommend the company's product and it's services
- Overall satisfaction with the relationship
- Overall satisfaction with the organization
- Intention to continue using the company's products and services

We assess trust based on the following questions:

1. Do they listen carefully with empathy and compassion? Do they question and involve the customer or stakeholder in a dialogue?

2. Do they communicate using clear, concrete and conversational language?

3. Are they honest and transparent?

4. Are they consistent, predictable, and reliable?

5. Do they act in the best interests of customers, stakeholders, and the public?

6. Are they careful to do the right thing? If they make a mistake, do they fix it?

7. Do they deliver on their promise?

8. Do they commit to the long term?

How you answer these questions can change the trajectory of your career and your company. These are the questions customers ask themselves when they are deciding to trust you and your company.

If this sounds simple and looks remarkably simple, it is, in theory. However, it requires levels of discipline and deliberate actions that few companies and people can mobilize or marshal. It is both simple and complex, readily understood yet profound.

Trust is created when the customer is at the core. Building, strengthening, and protecting trust begins with creating a customer centric trust culture. That starts at the top with the owner or the CEO and the leadership team. When leaders value trust and communicate it across the entire company trust building gets embedded into the culture and permeates throughout the company. When these foundational elements are in place, specific methods of communicating, behaving, and serving contribute to building, strengthening and protecting trust.

We can now objectively demonstrate the correlation between trust and profit. This means organizations can benchmark it, develop strategies to address trust gaps and measure again. The powerful stories in this book illustrate the results companies have had when they center and operationalize these principles in their organizations.

Throughout the book, you will see that I've included frameworks and tools for you. I've also included a few links if you want to dive in deeper. Here is the first one. To assess your team's readiness, visit https://www.successthroughtrust.com/trusted   to   download your complimentary *Customer Readiness Checklist*.

"When we listen carefully with genuine curiosity, take the time to understand the situation, ask questions to understand the other's perspective and show that we sincerely care, the impact can be enormous."

-Natalie Doyle Oldfield

Listen Carefully, With Empathy and Compassion, Question and Involve

Everything was going great for "Amy", until it wasn't. As she relayed the story to me later, she will never forget the Tuesday senior leadership team meeting when it all happened. The company's largest client was threatening to move its business to another provider. Because of someone on Amy's team.

Amy led a team of 45 technology professionals and was part of the Senior Leadership Team at a cybersecurity company. The team managed networks for companies around the world. Their largest client and its affiliated companies, representing approximately 25% of the firm's annual revenue, complained to Amy's CEO about a senior engineer on her team. The client said the engineer, "Bob", "had a cavalier attitude and was short with our technicians and senior leaders." They went on to say that they did not want Bob on the account "if his attitude and communication skills didn't improve."

Bob, the senior engineer they were complaining about, is a brilliant engineer and Amy and the company relied heavily on him. Bob was the most qualified to fix any significant network breach or security problem. The company had invested heavily in him, and he had several networking and security designations.

Annoyed and somewhat dumbfounded, Amy knew they had to tread lightly with Bob. They needed Bob's technical expertise; however, Amy also knew she couldn't be on every client call and meeting to supervise this talented but problematic employee. Nevertheless, Amy told the client's CEO she'd look after the problems Bob was causing.

Amy shared the clients' complaints with Bob, who felt terrible about causing trouble for the firm. Bob cared about clients, loved the company, and wanted to succeed. Along the way, Amy had heard from a friend in another company about an engineer who had learned 'soft skills' and communication skills in the Trusted Mastery Program. Amy enrolled Bob along with 9 other client-facing security operations and network specialists.

Amy didn't want to be blindsided again and knew everyone could benefit from learning how to build and foster client relationships. At heart, she wished everyone cared as much about the client as she did. So, Amy and I met and reviewed professional development objectives for each of the 10 people in the program. She asked that I work on Bob's 'soft skills', specifically his communication, listening and empathy skills.

The Trust Mastery program transformed Bob.

Before the program, Bob had many of the characteristics of a poor listener. Wanting to be efficient, he responded and jumped to conclusions too quickly, answered emails and texts during client meetings, and tried to solve problems before hearing the entire situation. In fact, he said, "all the problems are the same, I know what they [the clients] are going to say." Sometimes he asked closed-ended questions for no apparent reason, which clients and colleagues felt were wasting their time.

Even Bob's wife said he was a poor listener, but assumed he behaved differently at work. During the program, we worked on cultivating and improving Bob's listening skills. Listening is a required skill to build trust. As he got better at listening, he began to see customers and understand their perspective.

It was like a light bulb turned on for Bob. He had an epiphany.

Essentially, Bob learned that he wasn't simply fixing or managing a network. He learned he was looking after a network for *people*, people with lives and feelings, just like him, people who wanted to be heard and respected. Clients weren't a 'ticket number', they didn't want to be treated like a number, they were people who wanted a relationship, to collaborate and partner with Bob's company.

When we spend time thinking about a client's situation from the client's point of view, about the journey they are on with us, the landscape changes. Bob started appreciating the situation, his role, and the importance of the client to the company.

To quote Amy, "the change in Bob's behaviour is palpable. Colleagues and clients are noticing." "Bob now approaches colleagues and clients with patience, compassion and respect," she said. Bob "is now looking for and asking about ways he can help. He has become a trusted advisor."

I coined the term *'sales sensitivity'* to describe someone, regardless of their role, who is always on the lookout for sales opportunities.

Eight weeks after the complaint, the client called the CEO and the account manager to thank them. According to the CEO the client said, "I don't know what you said to Bob, or what you did, but my team tells me he is a pleasure to work with. A changed man. He's genuinely interested in working with us and getting to know the team. We don't know what you did but it's working. He's recommended a new service to the team that we'd like to discuss. We appreciate your fast action and want to talk about outsourcing more services to your company."

Amy was celebrated in the next senior leadership team meeting. She was relieved and proud of her team and of Bob. Everyone on the team improved. Six months later, Amy and the account manager met with the client and signed a new three-year managed services contract.

> *When we listen carefully with genuine curiosity, take the time to understand the situation, ask questions to understand the other's perspective and show that we sincerely care, the impact can be enormous.*

Step one to building a relationship of trust is connecting, showing that we understand, and we care. We must always be involving and engaging customers in conversations that affect them. This starts with listening. Customers are people, they love talking about themselves, and love sharing their perspective and their experiences.

Harvard neuroscientist Jason Mitchell and Princeton psychologist Diana Tamir completed several studies that found that disclosing information about the self is intrinsically rewarding. According to Mitchell and Tamir, people devote about 30- 40% of their speech to sharing their experiences and telling others how they think or feel about something. Their studies sought to identify what drives this behavior.

The neuroscientists monitored the brain activity of participants when they were talking about themselves. They found increased activity in brain regions that form the mesolimbic dopamine system. These are the same regions of the brain that are activated by the primary rewards of sex and food. The study also showed participants were willing to forgo money to think and talk about themselves. According to Mitchell, "We will often go to comic lengths to avoid talking about others and to keep the focus on us."[5]

The more you listen, the greater the impact you have. You learn what's really going on by diving deeply to truly understand the other person's perspective. Listening shows respect. You'll earn the right to collaborate, work with and advise your customer, colleague, or partner. Listening and connecting leads to mutual understanding and respect. The more I understand you, the more

I am familiar with you, the more open I am to collaboration, and to sharing. Philosopher Jiddu Krishnamurti said it well:

"If you are listening to find out, then your mind is free, not committed to anything; it is very acute, sharp, alive, inquiring, curious and therefore capable of discovery."

There are three key elements of listening: sincerity, curiosity, and genuine interest. Adopting all three will have a positive impact on your business and your relationships.

Empathy is the ability to recognize, understand and appreciate what others may be feeling and thinking. Simply put, it's the ability to see another person's perspective. When we feel in tune with someone, when we feel understood and validated, our emotional bond strengthens, we feel safe, the other person is more apt to work with us and to purchase our products and services.

When you are listening with empathy, you are actively sensing another person's situation including feelings, concerns, and paralinguistic non-verbal cues. Empathy is an extension of listening. It allows us to connect with other people and often engenders compassion and kindness. We cultivate trust when we show how much we care.

Empathy is the one skill that can quickly move the needle. Empathy is the cornerstone of smart leadership and becoming a trusted advisor. This is what transformed Bob. He became self-aware, he learned to connect, probe, and listen for the story, to understand the client's situation and to rid himself of distractions. He stopped listening to respond. His clients got comfortable talking about how they felt about a situation, or a project. Bob became more empathetic and compassionate and ultimately, more successful.

We've developed a tool called an empathy map, that we use with our clients. We fill it out together in the Trust Mastery program. We take the time to understand what a typical day in the life is like for the client. Then we look at what it is like to be a client of their company, we strive to understand the client's journey, and what the client is experiencing.

This approach changed Bob's point of view and shifted his approach to clients. As a result, the tone and his approach to clients changed. He learned a new process and it improved the customer experience.

Trust is the foundation required to deliver extraordinary customer experiences.

Ways to Develop and Show Empathy

- Listen actively and clarify. "If I'm understanding correctly…"

- Offer support, not solutions. Ask "How can I support you?"

- Reflect feelings and acknowledge their truth. "It sounds like you're feeling…"

- Demonstrate you recognize their perspective and gently reflect emotions back. "I am following you; I would feel that in this situation too…" ,"I would have asked the same questions …"

- Avoid judgement. Keep an open heart and an open mind.

- Practice patience. Give them time to express and explain themselves.

- Ask open ended questions.

There are many benefits to an empathetic approach, as Bob and his colleagues found at the cybersecurity company. There's no mystery in this. Customers are people and companies are made up of people. (For many of you this might be stating the obvious, however I have learned that it is not clear to everyone.)

Customers want to do business with people who understand them, who are compassionate and empathetic. We want to buy from people who care. And, we trust people who care about us.

When we feel compassion, studies show our heart rate slows down and regions of the brain that are linked to caregiving, such as feelings of pleasure and empathy, light up. The peptide hormone oxytocin is released when you show another person that you care or demonstrate compassion. Neuro-economist Paul Zak asserts "It's empathy that makes us moral," and calls oxytocin "the moral molecule." There is a lot of scientific data that suggest we are wired to care, down to the neurochemical level.[6] As Zak says, "In the brain the pathway for care, love and trust are all related to each other." [7]

The way we feel shapes our actions, our perspective and how we see others. Feelings matter. As the saying goes, at the end of the day, people might forget what you did or what you said, but they won't forget how you made them feel.

Once you have mastered the skill of listening with empathy and compassion, next comes questioning and involving your customer in a dialogue and or decisions that affect them. Like the Greek philosopher Socrates, I believe the customer knows the truth and by asking questions to understand their viewpoint, we will better understand their priorities, their wants, desires, and needs.

When I set about helping clients solve their business problems, my favourite first question is: "What is happening?" I follow this with a series of probing questions including: What is your perspective? How did that come to be? Why is that important? What else is important? Who else does it involve? When? What else have you considered? What else should we know? How does that affect you? How does it feel?" and so on. And when there is silence, I strive to sit quietly for a few seconds before asking them to 'tell me more'.

In workshops and coaching programs, we often show a picture of an iceberg. We know that we only see the tip of the iceberg, the top eighth. When you think about customers, consider that you are only seeing the tip and they are only showing us the tip of the iceberg. We need to dive deep under the surface, to get to know the person holistically.

Here is a tool to help you actively listen.

L – Leave the distractions

I – I am here for you, be present

S – Sit in the silence, silence is golden

T – "Tell Me More" is a powerful phrase and tool to signify that you want to learn more

E – Empathy and Emotions. Remember emotions lurk in every crevasse of the human organism, check your emotional listening filters.

N – Non-verbal cues: listen with your eyes and your ears

As an organization, do you listen carefully enough? Are you demonstrating empathy and compassion with your customers? Do you question and engage your clients and customers in decisions and discussions that affect them? Check yourself. Are you listening carefully enough? Are you present?

MAKING IT HAPPEN

1. Spend five times the amount of time thinking about your customer as you would thinking about what you are going to say or present to them.

2. Listen to others, to what they say, what they aren't saying and what they are trying to communicate. Notice their paralinguistic cues. Look them in the eye, show them how much you care. Give them your complete attention. Strive to make them feel like they are the only person in the room.

3. Be curious. Practice asking more questions with the goal of fully understanding their situation, their perspective, what is important to them and how they feel. Find out what is important to your customer, what motivates them and what really matters. Ask "tell me more."

"Clarity inspires trust."

-Natalie Doyle Oldfield

Communicate Using Clear, Concrete, Conversational Language

"Patty" was perplexed and somewhat frustrated. New leads were coming in, the team was meeting with the prospects, but the leads kept slipping away. "Clearly the work was out there, something is happening on our end," she told me.

As a partner in a national engineering firm, Patty was responsible for business development in her region. She was also busy with her own clients and had delegated some other client meetings to senior engineers and team leads in the firm. "Oliver" was the lead for the project managers and Patty wondered whether some of the problems arose from his leadership. Deciding to investigate, she started attending some meetings with him, in person and online. What she saw did not fill her with confidence.

Patty saw eye rolls, people slouching in their chairs, and frowns from the people involved. In Teams meetings, she saw heads down, black screens and people rarely looking at the camera.

From the all-important business prospects she saw pursed lips, very few notes being taken and even fewer nods of agreement.

Patty heard heavy sighs, mumbling and yes or no answers when questions were asked, often laced with tone. The team also would fall into using technical jargon with complicated explanations in response to straightforward queries from clients. As a result, prospects were not asking questions, or preparing for next steps. When they saw the team's cameras off, they turned theirs off too. Patty learned that the way the team was communicating was turning off people inside the firm as well. As a group, the team came off as arrogant and condescending.

Patty also grew concerned about how the team members were conducting themselves with current clients. She wondered about the effects on client retention levels, which weren't great. Patty worried about client meetings. "I can't be in every client meeting and or potential client meeting, but feel like I have to," she said. "I'm afraid of what they are going to say and how they will say it," she said. "The team isn't communicating what we do well."

Patty worked with a team of brilliant and talented engineers and project managers, but their behaviour and the way they were communicating was turning off new leads.

Most of us consider ourselves to be "self-aware," however the reality is many of us are not. We're not always aware that everything we say and do communicates a message, which is either building trust or eroding trust.

Clarity inspires trust.

First we decide to trust, then we look at capabilities. As Patty's team learned, if the firm's excellent capabilities were to matter, the sales prospects needed to trust her people first. And that was why the leads were slipping away.

Patty enrolled Oliver and his team in the Trust Mastery Program. They were motivated to improve their sales closing ratio and wanted to become trusted advisors.

They quickly learned to appreciate the significance of the old saying,

"What you do speaks so loudly, I can't hear what you are saying."

Everything the prospect sees and hears communicates a message and everything you say and do communicates a message. Sometimes it's what is not said that communicates the biggest message.

Consider the facts:

- It's been widely documented that it takes seven seconds to make a first impression.[8]

- 80 to 90 % of a first impression is based on trust and confidence, according to research by Dr. Amy Cuddy, a social psychologist at Harvard University. This holds true across cultures. [9] Cuddy also found that people respond more positively to someone who is trustworthy rather than confident.[10]

- The amygdala, an area in the brain associated with emotions and decision-making, makes a subconscious judgement about the trustworthiness of a face within 33 milliseconds of exposure.[11]

- Research subjects didn't recall seeing faces, but their amygdalas reacted differently depending on the face details.[12]

- A duo of Princeton scientists Nikolaas Oosterhof and Alexander Todorov found that certain facial characteristics connote trust. In particular, mouth and eyebrow shapes are important. Angry-looking eyebrows and downturned mouths are considered untrustworthy. More trustworthy faces have slightly surprised looking eyebrows and a smiling U-shaped mouth. [13]

The most significant factor influencing perceived trustworthiness is emotional expressivity, and it functions unconsciously. Therefore, to make a positive first impression, start with a smile. It is the universal sign of happiness and puts everyone at ease. Be confident and look the other person in the eye. Looking the other person in the eye builds trust.

As we discuss in our workshops and programs, if you aren't a natural smiler, which includes half the population, intentionally start your conversations with a smile. A genuine smile. We all know what a fake smile looks like, and fake insincere smiles erode trust. You don't have to smile with your teeth to be smiling. When you are genuine, it triggers the release of oxytocin in the observer's brain, which helps to calm their fight-or-flight response.[14]

Neuroscientists suggest we are wired to make decisions and process threats in terms of our own immediate survival. The brain's primary defense system, the amygdala is constantly looking for threats. When people are stressed, they go into a fight or flight posture.[15]

Your prospect is subconsciously assessing and asking: Can I trust this person, Am I safe with them, Is it dangerous to trust this person? Will I be able to work with them? Will the project be safe with them? Will it pose a threat to me if we work together? What are their intentions?

Keep in mind that people tend to personalize a crisis. A crises can come in many shapes and sizes. Your prospect might consider it a crisis that they have to choose an engineering firm to design a new HVAC system for their office renovation for example. If the prospect does not choose the right firm, they could lose their job. If the firm doesn't perform well, the prospect could lose their bonus.

When a prospects trusts, they feel hopeful, curious, creative, generous with their time and what they are willing to share with you. You can see and feel it in their behaviour. They are open and forthcoming with information; collaborative and engaged in a conversation; offering ideas and information and support. They are looking forward to the best possible outcome.

On the Other Hand:

When a new lead or prospect distrusts, they don't feel safe. They likely feel the need to protect themselves, which leads to fear, anger, skepticism and feeling they may not be able to handle what the other person might do. You can sense that they are not comfortable, which can show up in them resisting new information, criticizing, judging, avoiding, repeatedly asking for more detail, withholding information, and asking for information in writing.

As we discussed in the introduction, when someone is assessing our trustworthiness, they are evaluating how we apply the principles to each interaction. We trust what we understand and what we believe. If we don't believe, we probably do not or will not trust.

It Matters How You Say It

The believability of the message in-person comes down to the verbal, the vocal and the visual. In his book *Silent Messages*, psychologist and researcher, Dr. Albert Mehrabian taught the importance of verbal and non-verbal communication. His research revealed that only 7% of all communication is done through the words we speak (verbal communication), whereas the nonverbal components of our communication, (the 'paralinguistic cues' as they are known) the tone, volume, and pitch of our voices (vocal) make up 38% of the message; and everything you see (visual) from the facial expressions, posture, gestures make up 55% of the message.[16]

The delivery of the message matters. When it comes to building trust, how we deliver a message can be as important as the content. A confident vocal demeanor persuades and engenders trust.

When our body language and verbal messages are congruent, they inspire trust.

In the hybrid, virtual world, all the same rules apply. However, everything is amplified. There's a heightened awareness of your facial expressions on videoconference. So, it's important to show your face. In fact, I say "cameras on!" for online meetings, unless there is a good reason not to. A prospect or customer who sees a black screen might be left wondering, *what you are hiding?*

More and more people are communicating through email, text, and social media rather than face to face or by telephone. Remember, how you say it matters. Emotions matter.

Simplicity Builds Trust

Clarity inspires trust. We trust when we understand. When we don't understand, our eyes tend to glaze over, our minds wander, and we start down the slope of mistrusting.

Does everyone understand what you do? Here is a litmus test: Is it easy for customers and friends to refer you and your business? Is it easy for customers to buy from you?

The 2024 *Think with Google* study found "73% of consumers look for ways to make things simple when there is too much information available."[17]

10 Guidelines to Communicating with Clarity

Long-winded explanations, detailed descriptions, and complex arguments often confuse customers and can project evasion, fuzzy thinking, and disorganization. So:

1. Simplify your point.

2. Avoid vague generalizations and platitudes. Be specific.

3. Use concrete, familiar words. Avoid adjectives, qualifiers, buzzwords, acronyms, jargon and abstract terms.

4. Make only one strong point in response to each question. Do not try to squeeze in two or three points or too much information. The more you say, the less people will remember.

5. Support your points with examples. Good examples can capture attention, explain and enhance credibility more effectively than any other communications technique. Draw examples from personal experiences, things that happened to someone you know or heard about, history, something in the news, or a famous person's life.

   They can be humorous or serious. They can even be hypothetical: "Imagine how you would feel if..."

Ask yourself: "What example or story will clarify this point? Is there a story that includes personal details I can share?" As discussed in Principle #1, sharing personal details cultivates trust.

6. Make messages easy to visualize. According to plentiful studies, 55 % to 65% of people learn visually. Facts and abstract statements are not easy to visualize. Metaphors are an effective way to package and clarify a message because they can provide comparisons and visuals. A word of caution however: make sure your metaphors convey messages that are aligned with your visuals and make the right comparisons with you and your organization. You must be consistent.

   Images can help simplify, explain, and remember points. Images include charts, infographics, pictures, videos, and conventional graphics. As the saying goes. "A picture tells a thousand words."

7. Use simple numbers and statistics, not many. People trust numbers. We accept numbers as facts. Numbers can simplify, clarify and convince. But use them sparingly; too many numbers can confuse. Limit the numbers and statistics you use to two or three in each message. Convert large numbers into simple percentages to round them off.

8. Divide your message into three parts: effective communicators often clarify some of their messages by breaking them into three parts. This technique allows you to quickly organize and simplify responses to broad and complex questions so that customers

will understand and pay more attention to them. For example:

- Point out three challenges facing the organization.

- Give three reasons for supporting the decision.

- Cite three features of the product.

- Present three choices for consideration.

- Propose three initiatives.

- Plan three phases.

- Describe three advantages to the plan.

- List three priorities for next year.

- Make three important points.

You may ask, what if there are more than three examples? You can still use this technique by saying: "Three priorities, challenges, opportunities etc.," "I want to mention three points" or "The three most important issues are..."

Now that you are aware of this technique, you will be surprised how often you notice it being used. Hundreds of the Trust Mastery graduates will attest to its effectiveness.

9. Support your points with facts and quote independent authorities. Projecting credibility begins with telling the truth. Having said this, you can add credibility by supporting your points with facts and evidence

and quoting independent sources and respected authorities. Avoid offering an opinion when you can cite a fact that will make the point for you.

10. Tell a story.

In addition to these guidelines, go to https://www.successthroughtrust.com/trusted to download words and phrases that erode or cultivate trust.

MAKING IT HAPPEN

1. Show people who you are. After a client asked him how old he was, Mark, a software engineer, put his framed professional certificates and university degrees on the walls of his office so everyone could see them. He added a shelf and placed photos of his children in picture frames that his clients could see when he was in virtual meetings. He added certifications, professional designations, and diplomas to his LinkedIn profile and attached his designations to his email signature. Everything we see communicates a message.

2. Let your clients get to know you. After two prospective customers implied to the sales team that they didn't think their company had experience in manufacturing, the flag was raised. They didn't feel like they were perceived as credible or authoritative in the eyes of the prospective customers. To address this trust

issue, they invited prospects to visit their operation, to see the plant and meet the people. They placed pictures of the plant and the company from the past eighty years in the lobby and throughout the facility, added customer logos and customer testimonials to their website, created a 'capabilities sheet,' and an explainer video. They added customer references and the company story in their proposals, and a hired a videographer to interview key employees.

3. Adopt the shopkeeper's creed: Smile. Look people in the eye. Making eye contact builds trust.

"Nothing builds trust like the truth."

-Natalie Doyle Oldfield

Be Honest and Transparent

"George", the owner of a manufacturing company, had been on a long search for an ERP system to manage inventory, provide accurate reports, and integrate with the firm's accounting software with the goal to increase efficiency.

After carefully deciding on a vendor, George's team went through months of turmoil and disruption to integrate the new system. It wasn't as seamless as the vendor said it would be. George felt the vendor misrepresented the product by exaggerating its ease of implementation.

George wondered if the pain was worth it and thought the software's vendor could have managed his experience differently. George said, "I just wish they were honest and sincere. If we had known it would be so chaotic, we would have added more staff to assist with the implementation."

Some people think being open and transparent betrays weakness. They don't want to tell the customer they need more time, that the software has limitations, the delivery will be late, or an installation can't take place as scheduled because the customer didn't do their part. However, honesty and transparency are forms of confidence and strength. Being honest means walking the talk and aligning your words and actions. George said he wished the IT company had been honest and sincere and had candidly shared all the requirements. "Honesty and frankness are key values in our company, clearly it's not the same for them."

Sincerity is the perception that you are honest and act with integrity. You say what you mean and mean what you say. Sincerity is being free from deceit, pretense, or hypocrisy. Your words and actions are consistently aligned. If not, and people start to think you aren't sincere, everything else becomes suspect.

Intentional deceit or omission, when uncovered, can instantly and justifiably cause customers to judge you as untrustworthy, even if the lie or omission is "harmless" and only meant to avoid causing distress.

The software supplier may not have wanted to admit that adopting their product wasn't as straightforward as turning a switch. George couldn't get past it. To him, it was a lie. He wondered what else they didn't reveal. What else was in the fine print? Nothing destroys trust like opacity or misrepresentation.

Research shows that people are likely to tell sixteen people about a negative experience, while they mention a positive customer experience to an average of nine people. [18]

George and his team abandoned the project. The company lost $75,000 in forecasted revenue for the next phase of the project. It has lost all credibility.

Nothing builds trust like the truth, the full truth.

More than 80% of business executives believe you can't have trust without transparency. In that same global study conducted by Economist Impact, more than half of the respondents' said transparency was the most important quality to build trust. 86% said their organization would be more likely to work with a potential partner that demonstrated transparency, accountability, and integrity in its operations.[19]

If you were surveyed, you would most likely agree. When I conduct workshops and training programs, I often ask participants "What builds trust?" and one of the top responses is always "truth and honesty."

Transparency is key to improving your business results. So what does it mean to the business owner or leader, who might ask *"How far do we take this? Why is it important?"*

Obviously, we are not talking about sharing proprietary information or information that increases risk for your company. Transparency is about sharing information that affects the relationships and the outcomes for the company.

One of the most significant current trends is our growing insistence on accountability from the organizations that affect our lives. We have become more critical, more skeptical of companies and their leaders and less deferential. As citizens, customers, employees, and shareholders, we want more information and better explanations. We want transparency. Symptoms of public distrust are the proliferation of special interest groups, regulators, ever-greater demands for 'stakeholder input', and high numbers of consumer complaints and lawsuits.

Many companies are unnecessarily secretive and needlessly withhold information, sharing it on 'a need to know' basis only. Obviously, every organization must maintain the confidentiality of certain information related to competitive, legal, personnel and other issues. Even so, building trust begins with management's acceptance of the fundamental notion that the more the customer knows about the company's plans, challenges, and activities, the better.

As we have discussed, transparency fosters trust, credibility, and empathy. When you keep customers and partners well informed, you are rewarded with customers that judge you more fairly and with more empathy. They are often willing to give you the 'benefit of the doubt' when and if things go wrong.

In contrast, secrecy undermines credibility, promotes misunderstanding, and generates suspicion. Information gaps lead customers to assume that information is being withheld intentionally.

Transparency has Another Benefit:

The more the customer knows about you and the company, the less likely it is for a single incident to affect the customer's trust. A well-informed customer can put an incident into perspective.

On the other hand, while transparency puts negative news into a broader context, lack of transparency magnifies the significance of negative news. If the only news the customer has heard about the company is negative, that's what will stick.

Proactive companies tell customers everything they want to know about the company unless there is a very good reason not to. They know that trust, understanding, and sympathy are fostered when the customer is well informed.

Here's an example, based on something I personally observed a few years ago.

A senior leader was responsible for a large customer project, in development for six months. It was the most significant account in the company's eight-year history. Things were going well until a junior engineer informed the team that he'd discovered a design flaw in the new software they'd been working on.

If they didn't stop and fix the problem, the customer wouldn't have the functionality they expected. The feature wasn't written into the original specifications. Everybody missed the flaw, which would knock the entire project off the rails, requiring four more months of development and a missed deadline for their customer.

Of course, the right thing is to inform the client (Principle #6: Do the right thing. Be ethical and fix things the way you would be proud of). This exemplifies acting in the customer's best interests (Principle #5) and demonstrates the need to set the right example by publicly acknowledging the initiative of the junior engineer who pointed out the mistake (Principle #3: Be honest and transparent with everyone). The company needed to inform the customer (Principle #1: involve the customer in discussions and decisions that affect them) and get the project back on track. Such news must be communicated clearly and with empathy (Principle #2) as it could be an emotionally charged discussion.

In this case, the senior leader was upfront and honest. They shared the whole situation and how the team was going to resolve it with the customer. They followed the guidelines in Principle # 6.

The customer was understanding, and the team leader's actions built more Trust Equity™ with the customer. When we point out a mistake or an issue, it enhances collaboration and increases trust.

Many customers value honesty above everything else. When we are honest and upfront and openly share negative or sensitive news, it can be disarming. However, if you are transparent, the customer will be more forgiving if something goes wrong. The longer we wait to tell the truth, or share it, the more difficult it usually is for both parties to handle, and the bigger an issue can become.

Another way to demonstrate transparency is to communicate your awareness of the impact on others, even if it's negative, when making decisions or taking actions. (Remember we all want the truth, good or bad.) Explain the rationale behind your actions and clarify the interests they serve. You can never go wrong when you act in the customer's best interests and act with integrity.

Honesty is Key

Here is a scenario to consider: Which person do you trust more? The person who knows the answer to every single question, or pretends to, or the person who is confident enough to say, "I don't know." We build trust when we admit we are human, that we don't know everything. Ask yourself, do you trust someone who tells you everything is perfect, all the time?

Customers want to know the whole truth, good or bad. When something is too perfect, our inner alarms go off. We ask: "how could that be?" Vagueness, 'dancing around' a topic, exaggerating and sugar coating set off those alarms too.

Authenticity is key. One of the most common questions I'm asked is "how does a leader build trust with her/ his /their team quickly? Or with a customer quickly?" Here's my advice:

Be the first to extend trust. During uncertainty, before people really know each other, show them your genuine self. Be vulnerable. It might be difficult, but they will appreciate it.

Trust is created in the moments when people are being genuine, when they are open, honest, and vulnerable.

Show people the real you.

There is an important caveat to this. It takes discipline and self-awareness to understand what to share, what not to share, and with whom. We all know someone who "overshares."

According to researcher and professor, Brené Brown of the University of Houston, "Vulnerability is not oversharing, it's sharing with people who have earned the right to hear our stories and experiences. Vulnerability is not weakness; it's our greatest measure of courage." [20]

Here are some ways to demonstrate this: Let clients know you don't have all the answers, or that you are unsure how to do something, or that you made a mistake and are working to fix it.

Trust and AI

Trust is becoming more important every day with the massive changes in society and technology we are all experiencing. In an era of artificial intelligence, the need for strong Trust Equity™ will be more important than ever. AI is a multiplier, making it easier to spread untruths or impersonate trustworthiness. Thankfully, we can often detect foul play.

We humans have well developed "spidey senses." This intuition sets off alarms and tells us when something isn't right. The "tell" could be a word missing, a spelling mistake, audio and video out of sync or odd images in a photo. Offering greater visibility into how you or your business is using AI can deepen trust.

Who posted the information matters as much as what is said. Examine who said it. Is the source trustworthy? Did Chat GPT or some other AI program create it? In the social media and AI age, trust is more important than ever before. *Is the source trustworthy?*

Handling Customer Skepticism, the Right Way

Do you have customers who question or doubt what you say? Are they excessively critical and judgemental? Do they make you feel like you are on trial?

Relying on judgments and making assumptions can be harmful. This danger can be avoided by taking time to understand the situation fully. As mentioned in the last chapter, we are wired to make snap judgements about people. With time and empathy this changes, however some customers are critical and skeptical.

If a customer is judgemental and critical ask yourself:

- Is it because they don't understand?
- Are they criticizing because they are afraid or stressed?

- Are they acting like this because it is something they don't like?

- How can you educate them?

- How can you make your customer feel more comfortable?

There's a foolproof way to respond if you suspect your customer is being critical because they don't like what you are proposing or the outcome. Open the books, invite them to tour your plant, bring them into the inner circle, share the details, the complete list of materials, all the steps involved, how the commission is structured. Amazon does this well. If a package delivery is going to be delayed, they contact you to tell you why. They repeatedly share minor updates.

Being open, honest, and transparent reduces customer criticism and skepticism. This also helps manage expectations (as we discuss in Principle #7 Deliver on your promise.) Being defensive usually backfires. Instead, remind yourself: it is about them.

You know that feeling when you sense someone is not telling the truth? You suspect something is off, wrong, or just not right. Maybe you sense exaggeration, sugar coating, opacity, evasion, ambiguity, or indirect answers. Doubt and distrust are introduced. Distrust can also be introduced when someone is telling the truth but looks dishonest because they are uncomfortable with the topic (Imagine red face, fidgeting, eyes looking up or away, sweaty palms or foreheads). Ultimately, when body language is not congruent with the words someone is saying, we know something is wrong. People can detect lies. When this happens, inevitably, trust erodes.

Sometimes we are being truthful, yet it appears otherwise because of the way we respond to a question. We recommend identifying the topics and questions customers might have that will make you uncomfortable and scripting out your key messages. Then practice your responses out loud. Yes, out loud, not in your head. Everyone is different, what makes one person uncomfortable might not have any effect on the next person.

The following are examples of topics that make some people uncomfortable:

- Price increases or how prices are set
- Competition
- Dates for product updates
- Problems with a project or product
- Who will be working on the project or the account
- Missed deadlines
- Termination, dismissal, resignation of another employee
- Discontinuation of a product or service
- Commission, fees, compensation

12 Practical Ways to be Honest and Transparent

1. Share as much detail and specific information as you can.

2. Attempt to answer the who, what, where, when, and why on all issues that affect the other party.

3. Make honest claims about your social, environmental, governance, diversity, equity and inclusion initiatives. Do not overstate or understate.

4. Use artificial intelligence ethically.

5. Alert colleagues, customers, and stakeholders in advance of changes that will affect them including changes in personnel, product ingredients, bills of materials, pricing, shipping, delivery, lead times, return, warranty, or engagement policies.

6. Do not exaggerate or overstate the benefits of the product, service, proposed solution, or your capabilities. Cite limitations and make honest claims about the product or solution you are discussing.

7. Point out the pros and cons or the benefits and risks.

8. Outline agreements in one or two pages; avoid fine print, cumbersome contracts, and legal contracts if possible.

9. Develop explainer videos, documents, infographics, frequently asked questions (FAQ) for complicated and or potentially sensitive topics and concepts. For

example, how fees are set, how supply chain affects delivery time.

10. Declare a conflict-of-interest policy.

11. Create customer confidentiality agreements and keep confidences.

12. Create privacy policies and respect customer privacy.

Tools and technologies are available that can help keep customers informed. However, it always comes down to people. When customer-facing employees learn how to communicate and behave with transparency, relationships improve. You'll be rewarded with smoother projects, higher satisfaction levels, referrals and repeat sales.

Building trust with someone else starts with you. If people believe you're insincere, everything else becomes suspect. Are you being honest with yourself? Are you checking your intentions? Are you committed to what you are saying? Openness and transparency are building blocks of trust.

MAKING IT HAPPEN

Three Tips to Cultivate Honesty and Transparency:

1. Let customers know the full picture. Share the project plan: the timeline, contact information of project participants, the impact window, critical success factors and risks. Anticipate what people are wondering but are afraid to ask, or perhaps don't know what to ask. Whether it's team members or a customer, we all want to know what to expect, what's required from us, what's going to take place, how things are going to roll out and how long it will take.

2. Share your intentions and the real agenda. If you want to increase sales, retain customers, and gain referrals, sharing the real agenda is key. For example, if you are going into a sales call and your intention is to promote a new product, let the prospect know that's why you're there. If you tell your prospect something that truly isn't your intention, they'll detect this hidden agenda. Agendas with mutual benefit build trust.

3. Give proactive updates. For example, share upcoming delivery interruptions and how you are addressing them. Keeping people informed and involved builds trust and empowers customers and employees. For serious issues, the message should come from senior leadership.

*"Consistency,
predictability, and
reliability reduce risk and
the element of surprise."*

-Natalie Doyle Oldfield

PRINCIPLE #4

Be Consistent, Predictable, and Reliable

"Why aren't we closing more sales? We invest so much to attract new qualified leads; we get the leads… why isn't the closing ratio higher?"

My daughter Courtney, graduated from high school during the global COVID 19 pandemic. In September of her senior year, she applied to three Canadian universities. Within weeks, all three offered her early acceptance along with glossy brochures and welcome letters. Because of the pandemic, she couldn't tour the campuses. The buildings were closed. Everyone was working remotely. She really wanted to see inside the dormitories. She had seen the residences at schools A and B but it was the third one, school C, she really wanted to evaluate.

So we drove five hours to see school C. Luckily, we were connected to a recruiter at school C through a friend, and she really went the extra mile for us. She met Courtney off campus at a local coffee shop for two hours on a Saturday morning. They laughed, talked and shared stories about the program and the university. The recruiter showed her pictures of the residence rooms. We were impressed with her efforts and drove to campus to peek into the windows of the rooms.

The recruiter followed up by SMS text thanking Courtney for visiting. And that was the last she heard from school C for 3 months. In the meantime, schools A and B sent holiday cards, connected on social media, sent postcards wishing her luck on her exams, invited her to virtual tours, sent hot chocolate and stickers in the mail. At the end of January, all three asked for transcripts.

Even though she hadn't heard much from school C, it in fact was her top choice. In February, she confirmed her residence selections and sent deposits to her top two choices, schools A and C. School B was no longer in the running.

Meanwhile, school A consistently sent pertinent information and every time she asked a question, responded immediately. Over a 10-month period, they contacted her fourteen times. And I counted, because I was so impressed with their consistent effort.

School C responded occasionally but only after several attempts to communicate. Perhaps they thought, "We have the deposit, we've closed the sale."

They were mistaken.

In Courtney's view, the university stopped paying attention, providing value and building a relationship with her. She felt she would be just a number at School C. In her words, *"they aren't reliable, it's difficult to get answers, they don't get back to me, they don't really care if I go there. What will it be like if I go there? I'm not sure I can count on them."*

We make choices and decisions based on who we can count on and who we can trust. Not surprisingly, in the end, she chose school A: St. Francis Xavier University. St. F.X. took the time and made the effort to invest in building a relationship of trust with the qualified lead. And thus, closed on a four-year sale, approximately $80,000.

Consistency, predictability, and reliability reduce risk and the element of surprise.

Like compound interest, the company that makes consistent, frequent deposits ends up with the largest balance, the strongest Trust Equity™ and the new customer. At its core, trust is faith in the belief in the future actions of a person or company.

When a business is consistent, predictable, and reliable, we say things like:

- You can always count on them.
- You know what you are going to get when you buy from or work with them.
- You know you are always going to get your money's worth.
- They have never let me down.
- There will never be any surprises with them.

- It's easy to navigate their website, process, or support.

- It's the same experience every time.

Regardless of your role, whether you are the CEO, a customer success manager or sales engineer, your consistency, predictability, and reliability can have a significant impact on the risk and uncertainty a customer or prospect feels. Reducing risk and uncertainty builds confidence, assurance, and trust.

Neurobiology, Brain Chemistry and Eliminating Fight or Flight

Our brain chemistry affects our decisions to trust or not trust others. Many scientists believe it plays a critical role in these decisions.[21] By understanding these brain factors, we can create strategies to reduce risk.

Our brain plays a role in how we react to threats. Specifically, the amygdala is the part of the brain that reacts to threats. It scans the environment around us to identify dangers, triggering the 'fight or flight' response that works subconsciously, prompting quick decisions to keep us safe by generating feelings of fear, suspicion, and defensiveness. These emotions are linked to high levels of cortisol, a stress hormone. This response is helpful if there actually are threats present. When we act in a consistent, predictable, and reliable way, it reduces the 'fight or flight' response, it helps us feel safe because we know where we stand. The amygdala is associated with the formulation of memory and decision making.[22]

We all have emotional memory, in which our past experiences and interactions influence our ability to trust or distrust. And customers generally have long memories. Our past experiences shape our ability to trust or distrust. However, we can consciously alter the automatic distrust responses. By paying attention and practicing intention, we can calm this distrust network.

How can we do this? By being consistent, predictable, and reliable. By deliberately applying the Eight Principles of Trust. Simply put, if your actions and behaviour make people feel safe, they're more likely to trust you. Feeling safe means less fear and suspicion, lower stress and cortisol levels, and enhanced trust. When someone feels safe and trusts you, they can think and solve problems better.

Let's put ourselves in the prospect's shoes. What is the experience like for them? Often the company shares information; meets with the prospect to understand interests and needs; provides a proposal or price; and then waits for the prospect to decide. Some follow up a few times; most follow up only once or twice. Some organizations think that's enough, their job is complete, and they don't have to do or can't do anything else. The university we drove five hours to see thought this.

Consistently following up builds trust, even after you've completed a commitment or task. For example, when a client completes all the forms for their insurance policy, telephone to let them know the paperwork has been received, it is complete, and the application has been submitted. Checking in shows your commitment to them, which cultivates trust. When we repeatedly follow up and it's personalised, we reduce risk and uncertainty, making it easier for customers to buy from you.

Personal familiarity enhances this further. It demonstrates interest and commitment. St. F.X. sent handwritten notes to wish Courtney 'good luck on exams', reminders of important due dates, holiday, and graduation cards, at all the right times. 80% of customers say they are more likely to do business with a company if it offers personalized experiences.[23] Ultimately, people don't want to be sold to. We want to make our own buying decisions. As we mentioned in the introduction, people buy from people and companies they know, like and trust.

Authentic leaders exude a consistent and confident presence. They remain the same person each day, they're not always changing. When we're predictable and reliable, we reduce hesitation, threat, and susceptibility. In the Trust Mastery program, we see that establishing order and structure through consistent behaviour is exceedingly important to people with certain social styles. (For more information on this: www.successthroughtrust.com)

If you're the person who always shows up, you're sending a strong message. Customers, colleagues, partners, and prospects notice. Strong leaders and trusted advisors are relentlessly consistent. Customers crave consistent customer experiences.

In *The Power of Trust: How Top Companies Build, Manage and Protect It*, I wrote about traditions and rituals. They are effective ways to build, strengthen and protect trust. On the other hand, they also can be effective at eroding trust. When you make changes without warning or explanation, it can work against you. For example, if you break tradition by not attending a trade show or an event that you did for many years in a row, it introduces suspicion. Customers wonder: What is going on? Is everything okay? What does this mean? Changes and lack of reliability, when not communicated properly, introduce doubt, and can quickly lead to fear and instability. Any change upsets the proverbial apple cart.

In the virtual environment, consistency goes under the microscope. Inconsistencies that might pass unnoticed in an in-person environment are amplified. For example, we all notice the current time, displayed on our screens. If a meeting begins two minutes late, it might go undetected in person. However, it will likely be recognized in the remote environment. Not showing up for meetings or for your people can negatively affect the Trust Equity™ you've built. Consistency and reliability build trust in the leader.

The little things add up. It is easier and safer to do business with people who are predictable and reliable. Dependable follow-up shows you care that you're organized, and it reinforces commitment to the relationship (Principle #8).

Surprises are for birthday parties, not customers. Customers don't like surprises. Sure, we can be delighted with a surprise phone call, visit, room upgrade, coffee, or cake every once in a while. However, we don't want to be surprised with new information that affects a project, deadline or project.

Meetings and Agendas are Concrete Trust-Building Tools

Meetings are important and usually productive interactions, so take them seriously. Avoid cancellations or rescheduling if possible. Rescheduling makes the customer feel they are not as important as something else in your business. Let the customer know right away if you're planning to change the schedule, plan, agenda, or the personnel attending. Minimize surprises. As we have discussed, the longer you wait before passing on news, the more negative the impact becomes.

If you must reschedule a meeting, here are three tips to follow:

1. Give ample notice.

2. Let your customer know in person. If this isn't possible, contact them in the way they like to be contacted. Email is passive and an impersonal way to communicate changes.

3. Explain why you feel it necessary to reschedule. Trusted advisors and trusted leaders set agendas with customers and manage expectations. For more on managing expectations see Principle #7, Deliver on your Promise, which includes a tool to manage expectations.

When you take the customer through a high-level agenda setting discussion, you are setting expectations for what is to come. Studies show customers involved in decision-making, including agenda setting, are more engaged and positive about the process.[24] Consistency is a critical dimension to setting expectations. Everyone likes to know what to expect. Few like to be caught off guard.

Trust is cultivated through multiple interactions. As we've discussed, everything we see and do contributes to building trust or destroying trust. Trusted leaders provide predictable, reliable results and behaviors to the customer every time. They treat everyone the same, and are always the same person.

Ask yourself; are the uniforms, signage, reports, email signatures in your company consistent? Is the look, feel and layout of the offices, plants, and facilities similar? We all know what it's like to walk through Costco, IKEA, and Home Depot. The consistent and predictable layout makes it easy to shop, find and buy items. It contributes to its trustworthiness.

Is the product, packaging, and pricing consistent? We know what to expect when we buy coffee from Starbucks and Tim Hortons or a meal from Subway or McDonalds, no matter where we are in the world. These companies excel in consistency. They are some of the world's most trusted companies.

In the digital realm, according to Google's Zero Moment of Truth (ZMOT) study[25], a buyer needs seven hours of interaction, spread across eleven touch points, in four separate locations before they purchase a product or service. When seven hours of content and interaction are spread across eleven sessions in four locations, a strong sense of familiarity develops between you and your customer. People will get to *know* you, potentially *like* you and *trust* you and that, in turn, leads to *buying* from you.

People trust people with whom they have a history. Familiarity makes people feel comfortable. When there is no history, individuals often make connections via mutual friends, partners, or people from a common city, university, or organization. You might share an interest, a specific cause, issue, or organization. This transference of trust reduces uncertainty and risk. Establishing a common ground can create a sense of connection and ultimately a sense of trust.

Mistakes Companies Make that Frustrate, Introduce Doubt and Erode Trust

- Miss deadlines.
- Ignore, 'ghost' or fail to follow up.
- Give little or no notice when prices, policies, personnel, processes, and procedures change.
- Surprise us with a change in an agreed-upon deadline or timeline.
- Fail to set and manage expectations.
- Display changes in behavior depending upon personal moods.
- Say one thing to one person and something else to another.
- Show up at a time that was not agreed in advance.
- Fail to acknowledge personnel changes in the company that might affect customers' interests.

- Fail to inform customers of changes and when they do, do so only verbally.

- Behave one way in front of the customer's senior leadership team and another way in front of the project team.

- Avoid firm agendas, schedules, and timelines.

MAKING IT HAPPEN

Consistency Scorecard: Rate yourself, your team and your company for consistency.

This brief assessment will help you determine how well you and your company are doing.

This is not an exercise to get the highest score. It is a diagnostic tool to discover areas that need focus and improvement. Score the following statements on a scale of 1 – 10, with 1 being strongly disagree and 10 being strongly agree.

	Rating of yourself scale of 1-10	Rating of your team scale of 1-10	Rating of your company scale of 1-10
Interactions customers have			
Face to face & live virtual contact (videoconference) at networking events, workshops and courses			
Face to face & live virtual contact in sales, business development or professional settings			
Face to face contact in social settings			

	Rating of yourself scale of 1-10	Rating of your team scale of 1-10	Rating of your company scale of 1-10
Touchpoints - resources customers go to (or find) to learn more about your products and services			
Written content including sales sheets, brochures, articles, blogs, case studies, guides, testimonials, newsletters, downloadable resources, and books			
Video and audio content including social media posts, podcasts, webinars, demos, television, radio appearances, advertising, trade shows, and events			
Locations can be spread across a variety of online and offline places			
Offices, shops, plants, facilities, trade shows, displays, conferences, home office background, virtual backgrounds, video conference backgrounds			

Note: The interactions include in-person as well as live virtual events. Locations do not have to be physical. They can be spread across a variety of online and offline places such as social media sites or email newsletters.

Review your company's critical trust risk points and the moments that matter. Add those to the assessment. What other items should you rate yourself on? Add them to the list. If you want to take this a step further, complete the rating as if your customer or prospect was rating you.

"*Nothing reveals your motives and intentions more than acting in the best interests of others.*

Actions speak louder than words."

-Natalie Doyle Oldfield

Act in the Best Interests of Customers, Stakeholders, and the Public

On a frigid morning in January 2022, I met via Teams with "Madison", the Americas Director of Marketing and "Mark", the Americas CEO for a large manufacturing company in the health care industry. Their company had a problem: customer retention was declining, and customer complaints were increasing. The revenue forecast was unstable. Madison and Mark wanted to talk about the risk of losing long-term contracts.

Known for his laser focus and brevity, Mark spoke slowly, and his concern was evident. "We are a subscription-based business," he said. "We want customers to remain loyal for a long, long time. We need to regain trust and improve the client experience. Customer experience is part of our core mission. The last year (2020 - 2021) has been a roller coaster, we can feel the trust slipping away. If we could just focus on the things we can control – our relationships and the customer experience, we could begin to regain the trust of customers." Then he left the meeting.

Keep in mind 2020 - 2021 was the start of the global COVID -19 pandemic. The pandemic that seemed to change everything. It wreaked havoc globally, on everyone and everything: people, families, communities, and organizations. It changed how we lived, how we learned, and how we worked. The COVID -19 pandemic was one of the most disruptive events to business operations within recent history. It challenged supply chains, created unexpected changes in supply and demand, affected employee retention and morale, and delivery dates. And this company, like so many others, was not immune. They were hit hard.

I'll never forget the first thing Madison said to me: "Natalie, we need to know how bad it really is. We need to fix it. Everyone says it's a communication or a supply chain issue. It's not. We have a trust issue. We are known as the best of the best in the industry," and "we want to get that back."

Madison could see why they were having problems retaining their customers and she knew in general terms what was needed to fix them. "The (sales) team thinks they know everything, that they are trusted advisors, and they have no lessons to learn. Some large, long-term clients have left us, and several large accounts are threatening to leave. We need evidence-based data to help us make decisions. We need a strategy and a plan. Everybody is stressed out."

For Madison and Mark's company, contract periods are usually seven years. So, when customers started mentioning terms like: breach of contract, notice of termination or executing on a Force Majeure clause, the alarm bells sounded. The company's subscription-based revenue model for its equipment depended on customer retention, cross-selling, and upselling.

I arranged a call with the company's Vice President of strategic projects. They shared Madison and Mark's concerns and could see for themselves what was going on. "Silos are forming in the company … our culture is changing," they said. Employees were upset because the phones were ringing off the hooks with customer complaints. The field services and customer service teams were disheartened. The VP was overwhelmed and discouraged. "The entire team is working around the clock to help customers and fulfill orders," they said.

Here are some of the main elements of our discussion:

- Field services and customer services were not empowered to fix customer issues. They were not 'allowed' to discuss delivery times, warehouse problems or how equipment issues were going to be fixed. Only the sales team had permission to discuss those key issues of customer satisfaction. That had to change right away.

- Production and delivery updates were reactive. That created other problems that had to be fixed ASAP.

- The sales support and sales team would find out the company was going to miss a delivery date and would delay telling their customers until the last minute. Customers became furious, frustrated, and fed up. The salespeople weren't as proactive as they could or should have been.

- Employees felt like they were kept in the dark and they were stressed. Uncertainty and negativity always seep out from the source and infects others.

- The team was working remotely, and the management team confessed that maybe they could have done a better job making sure everyone was on the same page and in the loop.

- They had gotten away from sharing customer stories because they were so focused on putting out fires. This distance tended to impair the human factor in the sales-customer relationship, rendering it far less effective.

- Video conference meetings had become the norm. Before the COVID 19 pandemic, a customer would see someone from the company at least once a quarter.

- The mindset was "put a Band-Aid on it" and move on to the next problem.

As happens so often when problems start getting out of hand, fingers were being pointed and walls were going up. The Executive VP of Sales blamed it on supply chain problems and communications issues. As I reminded Madison, it wasn't a "communications issue."

You can't communicate your way out of a crisis. Regaining trust is about behaviour and walking the talk. How you behave says so much that people cannot hear what you are trying to tell them.

A science-based company by nature, they knew that a third-party objective view would allow them to see the forest through the trees. They invested in the Trust Equity™ Accelerator program to regain customer trust.

We kicked off the program with a presentation at the annual sales meeting. They wanted their 800 customer-facing employees to have the step-by-step framework and the playbook to rebuild trust with their customers, partners, and distributors.

Next, we surveyed 10,000 customers in North America using the Client Trust Index™. The survey uncovered gaps between customers' expectations and the company's execution. It quantified customer trust and established a benchmark.

The company learned the basis for developing a detailed action plan to improve the customer experience and regain trust. Through detailed segmentation analysis, together we gained invaluable actionable insights into:

- geographical differences

- differences among types of customers

- differences based on length of the customer relationship

Most significantly, the research revealed that customers on the west coast, who'd been doing business with the company for ten or more years, didn't think the company was always acting in their best interests.

You could have heard a pin drop when I presented the results to the leadership team. They seemed surprised, judging from their faces, and many heads turned toward the CEO, seeking his reaction to the news that their Trust Equity™ score was 72. Mark took the news in stride; however, I could see he was determined to fix it. "Now we know," he said. "We have work to do. Now we can improve and systematically solve this. We can earn back their trust."

Armed with evidence-based actionable insights, we devised a strategy and a plan to regain the trust of customers, elevate the customer experience and increase revenue.

Nothing reveals your motives and intentions more than acting in the best interests of others.

You can never go wrong when you act in the best interests of your customers. It might cost money in the short term, but in the long term you will win. We all want to buy from companies we feel good about and trust to put our interests first.

You might be thinking your company has a different business model and it's not set up to do this. I work with all types of businesses and the same rules always apply whether you're a transaction-based business, subscription-based business, professional services, wholesale, manufacturing, or something else entirely. Customers and clients want to deal with professionals who are trusted advisors, with individuals and firms that demonstrate benevolence. They want to buy from and work with companies that want to do good, even beyond where it rewards themselves. Companies that have a positive impact on people and the planet. Customers are paying more attention, and they are demanding more accountability; they want to see a social conscience.

Most companies I work with score lower in this area than they should. Improvement in this principle can significantly improve an organizations' Trust Equity™.

Essential Elements to Developing the Right Mindset to Act in the Best Interests of Customers:

Note: The most important part of acting in the customers best interest is doing it authentically.

- Knowing it's all about the customer
- Being curious and empathetic when listening
- Understanding the customer's perspective
- Having a serving mindset
- Believing in positive intent
- Demonstrating self confidence in your recommendations
- Showing sincere interest, curiosity, and compassion

Motives, intentions, mutual understanding, and mutual awareness are all keys to holding relationships of trust together.

Your customers and stakeholders are deciding to trust based on your past practices and plans to act in their best interest. This is how you can demonstrate that your motives are sincere, authentic and in tune with the customers' needs.

Business is always a transaction between people. It's personal. And when we distrust people, we engage in strategies to protect ourselves, like finding other providers for our equipment, withholding information, looking for mistakes and finding reasons to justify the mistrust. In my client's case, their actions resulted in an unintended breach of trust, which led to betrayal and loss of sales. This was never their intention.

As I mentioned to Madison, you can't communicate your way out of a crisis. Regaining trust is about behaviour, walking the talk. (Acting in the best interests of customers is part of the base of the Trust Triangle).

THE TRUST TRIANGLE

The large health sciences company did just that. They put words into action. We created a strategy to regain trust and they executed on the plan. They regained trust along with customer contracts and customer renewals. Within forty-five days, their revenue was increasing, and customer renewals were on the rise.

Here are a Some of the Concrete Steps They Took to Regain Trust:

- Created a KPI, measured Trust Equity™.

- Sent letters, in the mail, to all customers. In it they expressed their commitment to improve, shared the survey feedback along with the actions they were taking to regain their trust.

- Incorporated customer stories in the beginning of every company meeting and event. This is one of the best ways to talk about the company's vision, its purpose, and its values. They had videos of doctors and scientists talking about the importance of their products on patients' lives. As we discussed in the introduction, building trust externally, starts inside the organization with a customer focused trust culture. And a culture where everyone understands how their role impacts the company's vision and the customer's experience.

- Invested in cybersecurity systems to protect client data. They shared the security enhancements they made with clients and employees.

- Gifted every employee (3,300) three paid days a year to volunteer in their communities or with a charity of their choice.

- Invested in technology to communicate the phases and the status of where the product or service was in the process. They conveyed information about quality control, shipping, warehousing and whether their order was out for delivery. Similar to how Amazon and Domino's Pizza keep customers up to date with orders and delivery.

- Created a toolkit for their field services technicians, customer support and sales teams.

- Held guided discussions throughout the entire company on how to regain customer trust.

- Provided options and alternatives for customers on how to service equipment even if field services teams couldn't be there when they received the product.

- Placed personalized handwritten notes in product packages.

- Extended their hours of operation to provide an extraordinary service experience in all time zones. All frontline customer-facing people were trained and coached in how to apply the Eight Principles of Trust and they put the time into understanding and anticipating client concerns.

My client committed to their trust-regaining initiative. Focusing on trust is now baked into the corporate culture. They want to be the most trusted firm in their industry and are on a mission to provide extraordinary customer experiences.

The value of customer experience was quantified in a study of customers in a subscription-based and transaction-based businesses. In transaction-based businesses, researcher Peter Kriss found customers are likely to spend 140% more after a positive experience than customers who report negative experiences.

The results for the subscription-based businesses showed members who rated their experience as poor have only a 43% chance of still being a member a year later. This compares with a 74% retention rate among those who rated their experiences in the top two category scores. Customers who enjoy positive experiences are likely to remain customers for five years longer than customers who report a negative experience. Kriss also found that delivering a positive customer experience can reduce the cost to serve a customer by up to 33%. [26]

The Trust Accelerator Framework can transform your business, create extraordinary customer experiences, and accelerate your Trust Equity™.

Operationalizing Trust: 9 Ways to Act in the Best Interests of Customers

1. Have an internal 'code of conduct for responses to customers.' This could include responding to email within 24 hours, voice mail and texts before end of day or always picking up the phone by the second ring.

2. Deliver products to customers on time, even if the product is ready and the transportation company isn't. For several of my clients this means an employee getting in their own vehicle to deliver product.

3. Invite customers in once or twice a year to talk to employees about how the company's products, its vision, its values have touched them and made their lives better.

4. Recommend options and provide customers with alternatives. Make sure this is done when advice is sought, not before.

5. Suggest ways to save the customer money. You know a salesperson is acting in your best interest when they tell you "This is not the right product for you," or "you don't need that much product", or "you don't need to spend this much", or "a better delivery method would be ABC," or "you might want to try a different source" or "another company may have a better option to suit your needs."

6. Offer services or advice to customers without seeking compensation. While working with customers, you may see an opportunity for them to save time or money. Bring those observations to your customers' attention and you will deepen and strengthen your relationships with them.

7. Anticipate the questions your customers might have and answer them.

8. Provide tangible tools to delight customers. For example: No matter the size of the order, the sushi restaurant I frequent in Halifax always adds an extra roll. A life sciences company packs its product in dry ice. Every single box includes a note and a pair of gloves for customers. An engineering firm offers a complimentary strategy call. A food manufacturer sends aprons to its restaurant customers.

9. Measure customer trust. Make Trust Equity™ a Key Performance Indicator (KPI).

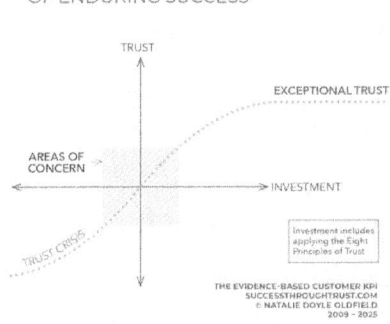

Note: This company's Trust Equity™ score was 72. When plotted, they were in an 'area of concern.'

MAKING IT HAPPEN

The Customer Champion Scorecard

This brief scorecard will help you examine your company's focus on customers and acting in their best interests.

This is not an exercise to get the highest score. It is a diagnostic tool to discover areas that need focus and improvement. Score the following statements on a scale of 1 – 10, with 1 being strongly disagree, and 10 being strongly agree.

1. Everyone is empowered, has clear direction on how to act in the best interests of customers, partners, and industry.

2. We discuss examples of what it means on how to act in the best interests of customer.

3. Employees understand the customer's perspective.

4. Employees understand the 'moments' and the experiences that matter most to customers and to our business. They understand the critical trust risk points.

5. When we make decisions and changes that affect the customer, we discuss how it will impact them.

6. Employees are empathetic listeners and are skilled at offering advice and options when it is being sought.

7. We are skilled at anticipating customer needs, issues, and concerns and are able to personalize the customer experience.

8. Employees understand our customers' industry.

9. We have a social conscience, we care about community and such issues as: sustainability, the environment, good governance, diversity, equity and inclusion, and issues that are important to our employees, customers, and the public.

10. We have a deeply held set of guiding principles and core values, code of conduct and ethics that drive every aspect of how we do business. This has been discussed and reviewed with employees.

Scoring Key

- a score of 9 or 10 indicates strength.

- a score of 7 or 8 is a good score but has room for improvement.

- a score of 5 or 6 is an area of concern, which needs to be addressed because if it heads in the other direction it could lead to serious issues.

- a score of 3 or 4 is in danger zone. This requires attention and resources.

- a score of 1 or 2 is grave danger. It and should be dealt with right away.

Go to https://www.successthroughtrust.com/trusted to download the Customer Champion Scorecard.

When you act in the customer's best interest, trust grows. Small acts can send big messages.

" *Doing the right thing is an expression of your values, integrity, and ethics.*

" *Nothing is more powerful than doing the right thing."*

-Natalie Doyle Oldfield

Do The Right Thing. If You Make a Mistake, Fix It.

'Turbulence.' That's the word "Charles" used when I asked what was happening in his large commercial insurance brokerage.

Customers were complaining, customer support time on the phone was up by 24% and customer retention was down. It was only down by 1% and to some companies, that slight decrease wouldn't be noticeable. But to this commercial insurance brokerage, it meant millions of dollars in lost revenue.

Charles and I met over Zoom. I noticed him in the waiting room, so we started 10 minutes early. Dressed in a white shirt and tie, he was twirling a pen in his hand and rocking back in forth in his seat. His concern was evident. "I don't know what or where the problem is," he said. "We are struggling to keep long term customers loyal in a highly competitive market."

He could see all the warning signs. "Customers aren't engaged, the sales team isn't either, and our channel partners aren't engaged. In our industry, customer retention is critical. We are losing customers faster than we are gaining new ones. The sales and customer service team says it's the industry, it has nothing to do with us."

Charles knew his firm faced some potentially serious problems. According to the global management consulting firm Bain & Company, reducing your company's customer defection rate by 5% can increase profits by up to 95%. On the other side of the equation, Bain & Company found that it costs 6 to 7 times more to acquire a new customer than retain an existing one.[27]

Charles and his company invested in the Trust Equity™ Accelerator program. They wanted an evidence-based diagnostic to quantify trust, to understand the customer experience, and correct its course. We surveyed customers using the Client Trust Index™ and found the Trust Equity™ score was 84%.

The brokerage served eight commercial industries. After a segmentation analysis, we uncovered a few areas for improvement. Customers in the construction and oil and gas industries rated them low in the 'Do the right thing' measurement dimension. Through discussions, we peeled the onion layers back and discovered that a few mistakes had been made on policies with clients and they were not fixed properly. Customers felt the insurance company didn't honour their claims. Several said people argued with them. A large percentage of customers did not always think the firm behaved ethically.

Charles and his managers had hired several new people, many of whom worked remotely and were confused as to what "do the right thing" meant in the context of their company and its customers. Through tailored coaching and the Trust Mastery program everyone got on the same page. We discussed their company values and how to apply them.

Nothing is more powerful than doing the right thing.

When you keep this top of mind, you can never go too far wrong. Doing the right thing is an expression of your values, integrity, and ethics. Ethics becomes part of the fabric of a trusted organization's culture. Everything we do reflects our values, morals, and ethics. Ethics are the moral principles that govern our behavior and how we conduct ourselves. Our ethics are rooted in philosophy. For deeper insight into the topic of ethics and philosophy behind it please consult my earlier book, *The Power of Trust: How Top Companies Build, Manage and Protect It.*

The insurance broker made ethical decisions based on their corporate values and by following the Golden Rule - treating others as we would like to be treated. In business and in life, we are constantly making ethical choices, whether we realize it or not.

Everyone on your team can take part in doing the right thing. Every employee can point out and fix mistakes and errors in a timely fashion, listen and respond to complaints, protect privacy, demonstrate ethical behavior, and empower others to do the right thing. As we discussed in # 5, values direct a company on how to behave. Communicating those values is vital.

So, to reward ethical behaviour, the firm started rewarding and incentivizing employees for sharing customer stories and wins that demonstrated the company's values. Sharing real, honest, meaningful customer stories with employees is one of the best ways to talk about your company's vision, its purpose, and its values. It also gives employees guidance as to what is ethical, what is the right thing to do at the company.

As discussed in the introduction, building a customer-centered trust culture starts inside the company, with everyone's shared understanding of the company's purpose, vision, and values. Leaders must lead by example. As Charles and I reminded the management team, if we don't, then the first time any employee sees someone in a leadership role violate those values without negative consequences, workplace trust is destroyed. We can't say we value one thing and do another. This principle, along with principle #5 form the base of the Trust Triangle.

In addition to rewarding ethical behaviour, Charles and the team invested in professional development. We created an onboarding and development plan for new employees and customer facing team members. They developed their skillset to become trusted advisors. They got involved in community events, including the local hospital fundraiser.

Over several months the number of customer complaints decreased, and the time to resolve them decreased. Within 12 months, customer retention levels increased by 2%.

Customers want to buy from companies that are authentic, that care about our communities, their employees, and their customers. They will support companies where employees and partners pay attention to ethics. They won't tolerate disingenuous activity or messaging.

Consider these facts:

A study by Pega Systems found that 70% think organizations have a moral obligation to do what is right for the customer, beyond what's really required. This same study[28] found that more than seven out of ten Gen-Z customers (born 1996 onward) are more likely to purchase from a company that contributes to social causes.

Sometimes, situations arise in which ethical questions can be quite complicated. Harvard ethics professor Joseph L. Badaracco suggests five basic questions for leaders to ask when making decisions in situations where the data and facts are unclear.[29] These questions can also help if you're wondering whether you are acting in the customer's best interests and when you're deciding whether you are doing the right thing.

1. What are the net consequences? Consider what the overall effects will be for everyone who is going to be affected.

2. What are my core obligations? Consequences are important but so are core human obligations. Some things are just wrong and are forbidden.

3. What will work in the world as it is?

4. Who are we? Test your decisions against core values, what the organization cares about and how it treats people.

5. What can I live with?

When You Make a Mistake

Because companies are made up of people and none of us are perfect, all companies make mistakes. When a mistake is made, we want someone to fix it so we're happy with the outcome and we have a good experience. When you fix things in a way that you will be proud of, often you gain additional trust. Often, it's about how the company fixes their mistake that builds or erodes trust. Here's a surprising fact about successful relationships: many were forged in moments of crisis.

In fact, sometimes we have more trust in a company or person after they've made a mistake because they handled it correctly, fixed it quickly and acknowledged the mistake in a way that built more trust.

Good apologies accept full responsibility, communicate sincerity, and acknowledge the person or people affected. Great ones are courageous and show vulnerability.

Here's a Checklist for Effective Apologies. They are:

- timely

- sincere

- empathetic

- compassionate

- accountable

- courageous

- show vulnerability

Bad apologies can be worse than no apology at all as bad apologies often destroy trust. Bad apologies typically do not address the issue, they blame someone or something else, they seek sympathy, they are insincere or take place too long after the event to be effective because the damage has already been done.

When Dealing with a Problem, Crisis, Mistake, or a Trust Issue - 10 Guidelines:

1. Acknowledge the problem and do it in a timely manner. Do not deny there is a problem when you know one exists.

2. Keep employees as fully informed as possible. Employees should be the first to know when and if

there is a problem, what has happened, and how the company is going to respond.

Do not keep the employees in the dark. Tell them forthrightly what is happening.

3. Be open, honest, and transparent with your stakeholders about any problematic situations. Inform your most important stakeholders first. Tailor the message to each stakeholder group as it relates to them. Do not be secretive about what is happening.

4. Accept responsibility. Be accountable. Do not avoid blame or refuse to accept corporate responsibility. Do not point fingers at any group of employees, suppliers or third parties.

5. Be specific about what steps you are taking to address the problem, resolve the issue or correct the mistake. The plan should include specific actions and timelines. Specifics engender confidence. Don't be vague about what you are doing to fix a problem. When people are vague, customers fill in the blanks and often make assumptions.

6. Act with urgency. Communicate the importance of the priority placed on the issue. Be as specific as you can be with timelines and plans. Do not delay unnecessarily before you act and communicate.

7. Acknowledge the impact of the issue as it relates to everyone it affects. Act with empathy and compassion. Do not trivialize the negative impacts of your mistakes or leave out any stakeholder group.

8. Realistically estimate the magnitude of correcting the mistake or issue. If it will take weeks, months, or years, if it will affect a lot of people or cost money, say so. Do not underestimate or minimize the challenge of correcting the mistake. We saw many examples during the pandemic of good and bad measures to deal with it. For example, some organizations blithely predicted the pandemic would be over in a few weeks when they really didn't know how long it was going to last. Admit what you don't know and ask customers and stakeholders for their patience.

9. Listen, acknowledge and address customer and stakeholder concerns. Seek their feedback and questions so you understand their concerns and fully acknowledge their seriousness. Collaborate with them to resolve the issue.

10. Acknowledge and correct all misperceptions and misinformation about a problem, don't ignore them. If you do, people will connect their own dots and will think the worst.

Every company should plan for a crisis. The plan should include: the list of critical trust risk points in your organization; a prioritized list of stakeholders; key messages for each stakeholder and how you will communicate with them. The plan should also identify your spokespeople and ways to monitor the success of the plan.

MAKING IT HAPPEN

Examples of Doing the Right Thing:

1. Honoring a warranty, service or return policy.

2. Following a code of conduct, or code of ethics.

3. Apologizing when you do not meet commitments.

4. Holding employees and colleagues accountable for acting in accordance with the organization's values, mission, and purpose.

5. Focusing on building empathy and compassion with customers.

6. Protecting the privacy of your employees, customers & suppliers.

7. Acknowledging and abiding by confidentiality agreements.

8. Admitting when you do not have all the answers, or if your product or service is not the right solution to solve the problem.

9. Acting on feedback you receive from employees, customers, partners, and or stakeholders.

"We expect to receive what is promised.

"Trusted Advisors and trusted leaders under promise and overdeliver."

-Natalie Doyle Oldfield

Deliver On Your Promise

"Steven", the owner of a 110-person cable installation service provider was out of ideas and getting exasperated. "We can't grow without engaged, motivated people! We can't find more people; we need to grow with what we have." "Most importantly, we have a multi-year million-dollar government contract coming up for renewal that is critical to our business." This renewal was vital to the firm's revenue growth.

It was the first week of January and I was meeting with Steven over virtual coffees on Zoom. Given the time of year, like many CEOs Steven was in planning mode. Yet he was worried. "There are so many new companies saying they can do the work that we can, that they can handle the volume, and that they do the best job. I fear that competitors are going to win the business," he said. He knew what the problem was: "We are so busy doing the work, that we don't have time to talk to customers. My team is exhausted, I'm exhausted. It's all I can do to keep the trucks rolling, get the gear in and get them to jobs. However, I know we won't win the request for proposal (RFP) and the contract won't be renewed if we don't start paying attention to customers."

Steven acquired the business in 2002, long before optic fibre and commercial grade internet were expected in every home, office, and hospital room. When he started in 2002, the business had one van and five installers. Through quality and attention to service the company grew every year. Today, they have a fleet of 85 vehicles and employ more than a hundred people. Their customers include government departments and commercial companies. They also have several competitors.

From 2020 - 2022, they installed and supported more fibre than they had in the previous 10 years. They grew so much so fast during the pandemic that the team was drained. As a result, emails took longer to be answered, installers grew careless with paperwork and some invoices got missed. Steven knew this had to be addressed or cash flow was going to become an issue. He'd been there before, having remortgaged his house to finance the business, which led to stress at work and at home. That was not going to happen again. He hired a capable VP of Finance and HR, "Melissa", who rose to second in command. Steven focuses on customers and operations; Melissa covers finance and people.

Steven was proud of his team and their accomplishments. But he needed every one of them to sustain growth and meet their ongoing commitments. The economy was experiencing a labour shortage. Skilled technicians were hard to find and even harder to retain, with intense competition for talent. The labor shortage had become the company's primary challenge.

When Steven and I met, a multi-year, multi-million-dollar government contract was coming up for renewal in ten months and the RFP would be issued within 6-8 months. For Steven's company, renewing the contract was vital. If they lost it, they would lose a significant amount of revenue, and several people would lose their jobs. But his team had been so busy that it didn't have the time or the energy to connect with the government's program administrators beyond the day-to-day issues.

We knew the company's installers, technicians and managers were great with end users, from homeowners to health care administrators. Excellent reviews were regularly posted on Google. But the end users were not the customers. The paying customers were a government department and commercial companies.

The cable installation company won most of its contracts through the RFP process, not through account managers or sales teams. Program co-ordinators handled the client relationships directly. This model had proved to be effective, efficient, and profitable. However the program co-ordinators were caught up in the daily grind and weren't planting seeds or tending to the relationships.

Steven tried to motivate the team to be more proactive with customer and stakeholder relationships, but many of his employees were indifferent to bonuses, company barbeques and gift certificates for jobs well done. Steven and Melissa decided to focus on rewarding employees with professional development. A 2022 survey of over 1,200 workers by The Conference Board of Canada found that 58% of employees would change jobs if they didn't receive professional development and training opportunities.[30]

Steven and Melissa needed a program tailored to their business objectives. Their primary goal was to retain their talent. Their secondary goal was to coach the team on managing customer relationships.

They decided to enrol six people in the Trust Mastery Group program: two supervisors, two program coordinators, an accounting clerk, and a project manager. Many had never had any leadership training, and a few had little formal education. Together with leaders from other companies, they focused on mastering the steps to delight customers and strengthen relationships.

Steven and Melissa had clear objectives for me to help them re-engage with clients and kick start momentum. After an initial assessment and some private coaching calls, I learned that people were working in silos, were not collaborating, and had become somewhat apathetic. They were so deep in the weeds they'd forgotten about what the company promised customers.

The program transformed the team. Here's what happened:

1. Steven's employees learned they weren't alone in finding it difficult to simultaneously manage client expectations and be proactive with them. They

learned from peers in other companies that their problems weren't unique.

2. They learned the government program administrators had become guarded and grumpy because they too were short-staffed and managing multiple programs, not just the rural cabling program my client was providing. (The empathy mapping exercise and tools mentioned in Principle # 1 changed their perspective). They realized that if they knew more about the government program administrators, they could better serve them. And they learned that the customer didn't know much about the cabling company beyond the number of installations completed each month.

3. By working together, the team could better manage client expectations and return to proactively impressing their customers. Together, they could develop plans to demonstrate their successful deliveries and the quality of their work. Significantly, they could achieve this and become champions of this initiative within the company. They resolved to revive their "can-do attitude" and rejuvenate the company's culture. Steve was thrilled.

Within three months of graduating from the Trust Mastery Program the project manager was promoted. According to Steve and Melissa, "He was a star going into the program, now he is rock star." "He is entirely focused on making sure the company delivers on its promises."

With new tools, the supervisors gained an appreciation and understanding of customers. They rediscovered their promise to deliver quality service. They committed to completing 'paperwork' at the end of each day, to speed up invoicing.

But it wasn't all smooth sailing. The company's accounting clerk was skeptical about the Trust Mastery Program and questioned why they were chosen to participate. The clerk was a long-term employee critical to customer relationships, who handled invoicing and billing reconciliation. Participating in the program with colleagues shifted their perspective and fostered empathy, particularly for the company's front-line technicians. They realized everyone was 'doing their best'. Collaborating with supervisors, they streamlined paperwork, enhancing responsiveness and expediting customer invoicing.

The two program managers metamorphosed right in front of our eyes. They realized that their customers were in the same boat as they were. They learned how to communicate with confidence. With a new empathetic view and new tools, they proactively started sending customer and supervisors inside the company biweekly status updates. They reminded the customer of their five-year track record of delivering on their promise. They were transparent with the government department, they began proactively sharing their virtues and weaknesses, and stories of challenging installations for difficult end users. They even explained why invoicing was often late. The relationship with the government administrators changed. As Steven said, you could almost see the shells cracking and the government administrators softening up. Both sides gained mutual understanding and respect.

Eight months later my client was awarded the contract. Their bid was 12% higher than the next closest competitor. Steve empowered the team. They worked together and they delivered on their promise.

Every customer wants what we promise to deliver.

Organizations demonstrate integrity and build trust by delivering on promises, by keeping commitments, behaving congruently with their values, doing what they say they are going to do and honouring their word. When organizations don't follow through on their promises, they are perceived to lack integrity.

If you say you will provide the highest quality fiber and best technical support, you must do that. When everyone in the company understands their role in delivering on the promise, you win and the customer wins.

Consider: what is your organization's promise? Is it highest quality, outstanding service, best user experience, friendly experts, largest selection of products, thorough advice or something unique to your situation? Employees want to deliver on the promises they make. When they deliver, it affects their performance in a positive way, which in turn affects the customer experience.

The transformation in Steven's team began when they began to feel empowered to wow their customers.

In *The Progress Principle: Using Small Wins to Ignite Joy, Engagement, and Creativity at Work,* Teresa Amabile and Steven Kramer reveal that employees excel when they make even small wins on work they find meaningful[31]. This underscores the importance of aligning company and employee objectives with the company's purpose and vision to foster a culture of trust. Meeting these objectives fulfills the company's promise, ultimately leading to a positive customer experience. Most importantly, when you deliver on your promise, customers reward you.

Delivering on Your Promise is About Execution and Results

Harvard Business Review noted that global CEOs identified execution as their primary challenge, surpassing innovation, geopolitical instability, and top-line growth. [32] Execution entails translating words into action and achieving results through discipline, action, and follow-up. We can have all the plans and good intentions in the world, but until we do something with it, it's irrelevant.

Research shows that tracking results and progress, and being accountable, doubles your results. Setting expectations by clearly articulating your goal is the first step in creating a culture of accountability.[33] Accountability is a key behaviour of a trustworthy person.

The Other Side of the Coin: When Expectations are Not Managed, and the Promise is Not Delivered

Managing price expectations is crucial across all industries and for every company. Here's an example of an instance when I felt misled, and how I responded.

I was working with an accounting firm that was preparing *Success Through Trust*'s taxes. I telephoned to follow up on an item he was asking about. I let him know that I was planning to sell my workbook, *Building Trust with Customers: A Workbook*, online. This took about five minutes. We then chatted about his recent vacation, my children and a business event that was happening in our city. The call was forty minutes in total. Thirty days later I received a bill for $600. The description was 'telephone conversation (40 minutes) and research relating to selling workbooks online.'

As we discussed in Principle #4, customers do not like surprises. We want to know what to expect. We trust when people are honest, open and transparent (Principle #3).

I was caught off guard by the bill and felt deceived. It changed both my sentiment towards him and my behavior. I simply stopped calling. I didn't expect to be charged to talk about vacations and children. It eroded the trust and drove a wedge in our relationship. When I saw the bill, I thought: "Why did he charge me for 35 minutes to chit-chat?" After three years of working with him, couldn't he answer one simple question? Why wouldn't he tell me that I was going to be charged for the entire conversation? Clearly, he didn't really care about me or my account.

The next year I emailed to ask how much the bill was going to be. Satisfied with the price, he completed the returns; we received an invoice, for $300 more than the original quote, with no explanation as to why. Again, I was taken aback. I did what most people would do: I didn't protest, I didn't complain. This time, like most unhappy customers, I simply found a new accountant. He didn't deliver on his promise, didn't care enough to address the situation, and didn't have sufficient Trust Equity™ with me, so I left.

Every individual's critical trust risk points are different. That's why it's so important to know your customer. In the example, the accountant failed to take the time to understand me, his client. When I asked him to call if he had questions, he would email. He didn't return calls. He never reached out to review financial statements with me; they were emailed. All of these little things were critical trust risk points and they added up. However, the most significant one was the bill. Twice I was unpleasantly surprised. Managing customer expectations is critical. None of us like surprises.

Ask yourself: do you raise the issue of price before your customers do? Do your customers know the total cost of doing business with you?

Identifying your Trust Risk points can take the 'surprise' out of the equation. When companies set out to determine their critical trust risk points, we perform a Trust Risk Point Audit. We identify critical trust risk points; assign a rating to each risk: high, moderate or low on a scale of one to ten; identify the specific actions required to address the risk; determine the timeline and identify who is responsible for carrying out the task.

As we've discussed, clarity inspires trust (Principle #2) and nothing builds trust like the truth (Principle #3). Consistently managing expectations cultivates reliability (Principle #4).

Managing Expectations is a Cornerstone Skill to Deliver on Your Promise.

When it comes to articulating expectations, there are three main components to address:

1. Time: How long will it take? Of my time, your time, and for the entire process? In other words, when will it be completed? Be specific.

2. Investment: How much will it cost? What are the fees? What internal resources are required? If there are no fees, then say no fees. If there is a fee, make sure you let the client know what it is.

3. Outcome: What is the expected outcome? What will we accomplish? What objective will be met? Be specific. When a component is missing, the customer loses confidence.

MAKING IT HAPPEN

In every transaction we subconsciously ask; will they do what they say they will? Are they who they seem to be? What is their track record? Do they have the capabilities to fulfill their promise? Do they consistently perform? Are they capable? What is it like to deal with them? Are their products and services up to date? Will we consistently get the experience we expect? Do they act in the way we expect? Can we count on them?

How would your colleagues answer these questions? How would your customers answer?

Ask yourself:

Does everyone in your organization know the key objectives, the purpose, the vision, the values, and the organization's promise?

"Reputation is about past performance. Trust is a predictor of future success."

-Natalie Doyle Oldfield

Commit to the Long Term

Like many manufacturers of building materials, our final company saw its revenues soar during the Covid-19 pandemic. People were stuck at home, renovating and remodelling and demand for this company's products soared, along with revenues. And then the pandemic ended, and demand declined, sharply, to pre-pandemic levels. For a full year, sales were flat.

This mid-sized manufacturer has a strong brand, a significant market share in its category and one flagship product. The company is well known for a couple of products and has the manufacturing capability to produce more. The company sold its products to distributors and wholesalers who then sold to retailers. They had a lot of supply chain issues during the pandemic, which resulted in massive shipping delays. Volume was down with their wholesalers and distributors, and they hadn't signed up a new distributor for a few years. However, the VP of sales reported that they were going through a 'rough patch'. The senior leadership team was concerned and realized they needed help.

It had to be all hands-on deck. Everyone in the company was asked to help the sales team.

However, nothing really changed, and they continued to struggle. They weren't coming up with new leads and after three months, revenues started to decline, ever so slightly but noticeably.

Then "Jane" and I met.

"Jane" the COO of the company in this example, was a member of a business peer group, where I had given a presentation. Afterward, it was my good fortune to end up sitting with her at lunch. She leaned over and whispered, "How do you get people more customer focused? We are going through a rough patch. Sales are flat. If we could just get people more customer focused, I think we could turn things around." Mark Twain once said,

"The only critic whose opinion counts is the customer."

So I asked Jane, what feedback she was getting from customers. "The VP of Sales says our customers don't think we're innovative," she said. The Sales VP "says that's why it's difficult to get meetings with our wholesalers and distributors (i.e. the customers). The first thing they ask is 'do you have any new products? Call us when you have something new.'" This, along with the flat revenues, were signals of low trust.

Jane's team felt overwhelmed. The company faced aggressive competition from new entrants offering lower prices for essentially the same products, not to mention pressure from economic fluctuations, inflation, and price increases from their suppliers. It was a squeeze. "We don't know what to do," Jane said, obviously worried. "We asked everyone to help the sales team, but nothing has changed. This is all affecting employee morale, which means it's affecting productivity and operational costs."

Jane knew in her heart what had to be done. "If we could get people more customer focused, I think we could turn things around. We're really working hard to maintain our strong reputation in the industry. We want to be seen as the most trusted in the country."

A couple of weeks later Jane introduced me to the senior leadership team and they shared their growth plans. They confided that revenue had been flat for the past eighteen months, they only had a few people in sales, and they felt vulnerable. We reviewed the company values and the critical trust risk points.

Based on that review, Jane and the CEO took action. They signed on to the Trust Equity Accelerator Program. We surveyed key wholesalers and distributors because the best way to find out what your customers want is to ask them. They responded, telling Jane and her team that they perceived a lack of innovation and a lack of commitment. Many did not believe the company was investing in the future or that it was taking action to demonstrate a commitment to them for the long term.

Jane and the CEO were surprised. The CEO said, "we have a great reputation! I don't understand. We've been around for more than 100 years!"

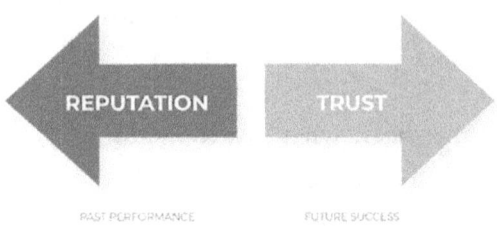

Reputation is about past performance.
Trust is a predictor of future success.

Jane's company knew that without engaged and loyal customers, there is no way to sustain a successful business. Realizing that the current sales group needed support if they were going to right the ship, they invested in key operations employees to become more customer focused. Eighteen people enrolled in the Trust Mastery Group program, including the CEO's executive assistant, the production manager, plant manager, engineering manager, continuous improvement manager, the supply chain manager, and several customer support.

Things immediately shifted for the company. Graduates of the Trust Mastery program became sensitive to sales. And, they became Trusted Advisors. They were encouraged and empowered to build relationships with customers and suppliers. They invited customers to tour the plant, they offered educational webinars for customers, and participated in more industry events. Everyone was talking about customers.

In thirty years, "Thomas" had never spoken directly to a customer. He was transformed, something no one saw coming. Thomas is not in sales, business development, or customer support. He is a technical expert, a plant supervisor, responsible for maintaining millions of dollars' worth of equipment.

His transformation began during a group exercise in the Trusted Mastery program and crystallized in a private one on-one-coaching call Thomas and I had after the session. A switch flipped when Thomas realized he knew very little about the company's customers. Encouraged to build relationships and learn more about them, Thomas asked the customer if he could visit. So off he and his manager went, to visit one of the company's largest customers.

What happened? In Thomas's words: "I gained a whole new perspective and new confidence. Because of your course, I asked to visit them [the customer]. The visit moved the relationship forward, and we are now collaborating on another project with them. I used the tools to prepare for the meeting and asked the questions we practiced."

His manager was thrilled, Jane was thrilled, so were the CEO and the customer. The VP of sales was relieved, and he was not alone. There are now eighteen people in addition to the sales team who are focused on customers. Eighteen people who focus on delighting customers, listening for ways to provide value and listening for new opportunities for the company.

Three months later Thomas and the account manager received a purchase order worth $2 million.

Nine months after that, Jane told me they had more opportunities than ever in their company's history. In fact, they had to create a new process to vet all the opportunities. They have developed a new product and revenues have increased.

In addition to the sales team and the graduates of the Trust Mastery program connecting with customers, the senior leadership team started reaching out and participating in industry events.

Everything you do makes an impact.
It either builds trust or erodes it.

Ask yourself, how often do you visit customers? Tour their facilities? How often do you attend industry events with them or sit in with them on project meetings? How often do you share customers' stories internally? Is the culture of your company as customer focused as it could be?

The lack of innovation, dialogue, and feedback had led customers to believe the company wasn't committed to the long term. The company had been resting on its laurels, on its sterling reputation.

After finding out their Trust Equity™ score and learning how to build and rebuild trust, the century old company has a new energy. You can feel it and you can see it.

Committing to the long-term means being enthusiastic and disciplined about creating a customer centred culture of trust. As Ralph Waldo Emerson said:

*"Enthusiasm is one of the most powerful engines
of success. When you do a thing,*

*do it with all your might. Put your whole soul
into it. Stamp it with your own personality.*

*Be active be energetic, be enthusiastic and faithful,
and you will accomplish your object. Nothing great
was ever achieved without enthusiasm."*

It is the owner's and the CEO's responsibility to set the company's purpose, values and vision and the operational parameters that create trust. All organizational trust begins with the leader (owner) and the leadership team. If company leadership doesn't believe and behave appropriately, the organization cannot sincerely build and cultivate relationships of trust.

Top leadership set the tone, however it's the people who interact with the customer who make it happen. The front line: the people in customer service, project managers, field services, account managers – anyone who interacts with the customers. It is everyone's responsibility to create trust from the corner office to the shop floor.

Everyone in the company needs to commit. First is the senior leader's commitment and choice. The second part is a commitment from the employees who make it happen for customers every day.

10 Ways to Show your Commitment to the Long Term

1. Adopt a forever mindset. Trusted advisors commit to relationships by adopting a long-term view to customer relationships. Strive to become a trusted advisor and commit to the long term. Trusted advice is a crucial part of how we decide to make a purchase. This is true in all businesses, big and small, whether we manufacture steel rods, service electrical substations, design suspension bridges or provide professional advice. Trusted advisors cultivate a partnership mindset to build customer relationships.

2. Have a vivid and compelling vision for the future, with a clearly articulated purpose and a clear set of company values that guide behaviour and organizational decision making. Fulfilling your purpose helps others trust you. Ensure that everyone understands and is empowered to apply these values, regardless of the size of the company. Trusted leaders make sure everyone on the team believes in the vision and knows the company's priorities.

An organization's purpose, vision and values must form the bedrock of expectations and behaviour for all employees. A focus on customers and serving them first is at the foundation of my model to build trust. The vision and the values guide employee expectations, behaviour and decision making.

3. Ensure that your colleagues and coworkers are as engaged, committed, and as focused on customers as you are. Check in with colleagues, share customers' stories and their challenges.

Engaged employees deliver customer experiences that disengaged employees can't. Trusted leaders and trusted advisors know that everybody in the company has a part to play in the customer's decision to trust. Building trust externally starts inside your organization, however the quality of a company's customer experiences rarely exceeds the quality of employee experiences.

Let your colleagues and co-workers know how important each person's part is. A Global survey conducted by the O.C. Tanner Institute found employees are eighteen times more likely to produce great work if they are recognized. In this same study 84% of employees said the simple act of giving recognition inspires them to think about better ways to get things done.[34]

At the same time, an organization built on a customer-centred trust culture will help "police" and coach employees who go offside. It is not just managers' responsibility to monitor how teammates are behaving. Everyone is responsible.

And don't forget remote employees. When we work remotely, we sometimes forget to celebrate the team's achievements and successes. While we may not be able to physically shake hands, there are other ways to celebrate our wins. Colleagues (like customers) have long memories. So celebrate the wins and demonstrate your commitment to them.

According to Gallup, chances of employees being engaged are only one in twelve when remote employees don't trust their organizational leadership. When there is high trust, engagement skyrockets to better than one in two. That's more than a sixfold increase.[35] Showing appreciation extends to suppliers and customers, too.

4. Thank customers. Proactively show them your appreciation. A handwritten note is powerful. These days, too few people send them. An audio message, a text, email, a voice message can be sent from anywhere any time.

5. Ask for customer feedback, through surveys, customer panels, interviews, focus groups, discussions, and whatever other approaches you can think of, to find out and understand what their experience is. It is essential that you spend the time, energy and resources to find out what their experience is, how to improve it and what an extraordinary customer experience means to them. Whether you do a formal survey using an external third party or carry it out internally on your own, get it done. The reality is, too many businesses do absolutely nothing.

Companies that understand their customers, outperform. A study by McKinsey showed that businesses that extensively leverage customer data analytics experience a 126 % increase in profit compared to their peers, and a 186 % increase in sales growth.[36] Measure customer Trust Equity™ and incorporate it as a key performance indicator (KPI).

6. Anticipate customer needs and look for ways to help customers and their businesses. Master trust builders and trusted advisors strive to think, support and advise as if they themselves were owners of their customers' businesses. Remember what is important to your customers, including the little things. Provide value and keep in touch long after the sale

is made or the project is finished. Share information, facilitate introductions and make connections, whether in person or online.

7. Strive to be a good corporate and community citizen with a social conscience. We trust companies that act in the public's best interests. Pay particular attention to the causes that matter to your customers, colleagues, and stakeholders.

8. Pay attention to the customer experience and the customer journey. Our association with a company is based on how it makes us feel and how we are delivering on the promise. Remember Principle #7, every customer wants what you promise to deliver.

9. Strive to be humble. Respectful leaders act in the best interests of their colleagues, customers, and stakeholders (Principle #5).

10. Pledge to continuous improvement. Committing to the long term requires passion, perseverance, and a drive to improve. Continuous sustainable improvement shows commitment, whether that is through professional development or investing in your product, plant, or service.

Walk the talk: If for example, you are committed to innovation, invest in it. We trust results, and we trust when people deliver on their promises. If you are focused on offering professional advice, make sure you and your colleagues are constantly sharpening your saw and that you're hiring the top talent.

Building trust is a journey, not a destination. As Aristotle says,

*"We are what we repeatedly do. Excellence
is not an act but a habit."*

The customer's trust in the organization is made up of the sum of the experiences they have with everyone in the company. We experience companies through end-to-end experiences, not touchpoints. We assess the trustworthiness on the cumulative interactions. This means every aspect of customer service, from the digital journey to retail ambiance, to hearing someone speak at a conference, or a visit by a technician to your home or office, to the user interface on your customer portal, even the way the bill or invoice looks.

As Nike founder and CEO Phil Knight said in his autobiography, Shoe Dog, the best advice he ever gave himself was "just keep going. Don't stop. Don't even think about stopping until you get there…" He gave himself this advice in 1962. And in his autobiography, he wrote, "half a century later, I believe it's the best advice — maybe the only advice — any of us should ever give."

My advice to you is to never stop building trust with your customers, employees, colleagues, and stakeholders. Never stop applying the Eight Principles of Trust to your relationships.

Committing to the long term starts with building a customer centered trust culture.

To download a poster to share with your team, please visit https://www.successthroughtrust.com/trusted

No one can do it alone and we all need a team. Research conducted by Google found the key ingredient and the strongest predictor of high performing teams is a culture of trust.[37] And high-performance teams outperform, for their companies and for their clients.

A strong culture can increase net income 756 % over eleven years, according to a Harvard study of more than two hundred companies.[38]

Bottom line: The customer's trust in the organization is made up of the sum of the experiences they have with everyone in the company.

MAKING IT HAPPEN

Make Tuesday and Thursday Trust Building Days.

Tuesdays with customers and Thursdays with a co-worker. Making allies inside your company.

- Every Tuesday, check in with a customer. Visit them, call them, leave them a message, send a video, or a note. Before too long, you'll see the dividends pay.

- Every Thursday check in with a co-worker. Connect with someone who helps you get your job done, or someone who supports you and helps you build trust with customers.

If you're in sales, start by connecting with the person in charge of pricing, or customer support or the person who prepares the estimates for the quotes.

If you're an engineer start by connecting with business development, shipping, or marketing.

It doesn't matter what your role is, nor does it matter where you start. There is always someone. Connect. Make a new ally. Build relationships inside the company. Companies are like machines, there a lot of moving parts and functions. Every part needs to work together and perform to deliver on the promise the company offers to customers.

"Everything you do makes an impact. It either builds trust or erodes it."

-Natalie Doyle Oldfield

The Art and Science of Being Trusted

As we saw earlier in this book, "Chris" the new owner and Chief Technology Officer left a wake behind him after his live question and answer session at the industry conference, but not for the best reasons. At the conference, Chris seemed to lack empathy and to be bored with the audience. He seemed dismissive and his interactions betrayed a lack of concern. By saying things like: "This is how it is going to be now," Chris introduced doubt and uncertainty about himself and the organization. He undermined trust in his leadership and therefore in the company.

However, most people in the audience didn't complain, at least not out loud. They spoke through their actions and choices. Like a slow leak, inquiries started drifting away, client negotiations went south, a few key employees left for other jobs and some long-term customers started asking questions about the company's future. The warning signals of potential trouble were surfacing.

As mentioned in the introduction, the head of marketing had seen glimpses of this attitude in the past in the company's internal meetings. They knew Chris lacked "soft skills." He "wasn't great in client meetings without another senior leader in the room," however, they knew Chris as a brilliant technical leader who cared deeply about the firm and its success.

Companies and leaders succeed not because they are smarter, or more agile. They succeed because they know how to build relationships of trust. The good news is, trust can be measured, learned, and improved. Chris did not have "it" – the ability to consistently build relationships of trust, to project confidence and trustworthiness. Step one toward fixing that and becoming a trusted leader, as we saw in the introduction, is to look in the mirror. Chris was not naturally self-aware and that manifested itself in the warning signals the company was getting, including the increasing number of clients questioning the credibility and performance of their product.

Trust is the foundation required to deliver extraordinary customer experiences.

Amazon CEO Jeff Bezos drove home the point when he said, "If you make customers unhappy in the physical world, they might each tell six friends. If you make customers unhappy on the Internet, they can each tell 6,000 friends."

Conversely, loyal customers help you grow your business. They evangelize for us through their social media, their offline interactions and with friends and family.

Chris had an awakening one day while meeting a long-time valued client at lunch. The client had been less forthcoming than he normally was, and Chris asked if something was on his mind. The client paused, then asked, "we were wondering under the new way of doing things, if we are going to be one of the ones in the know."

Chris was pretty sure his jaw dropped. Here he was sitting across from his most valued client, essentially being asked if their business mattered anymore.

It hit him like a gut-wrenching ton of bricks. His words and message at the Q and A session had sent all the wrong signals to his customers and industry stakeholders. It was hard for him not to take it personally since he had spent years dedicated to ensuring that their customers received the best in IT support in the market.

On the drive back to the office, Chris resolved to take the steps necessary to learn how to communicate with his customers, so they understood how committed he was to having relationships of trust with them. He wanted to be a Trusted Advisor to customers. Chris said he realized "I'm the root cause. Everyone around me is trying to do damage control. We need help regaining trust if this company is to continue to be successful."

As we've discussed throughout this book, trust is established, strengthened, and maintained through the sum of the experiences a customer has with everyone in a company. *Everyone.* Every employee has a part to play in the customer's decision to buy, to invest, to support and to trust you and your company.

We all prefer to do business with people we know, like and trust. The fact is that we decide to trust first, then we decide to buy. That makes trust the biggest barrier and the biggest enabler to your success.

However, it is the owners' and leaders like Chris' responsibility to set the tone. Building, strengthening, and protecting trust begins with creating a customer-centric trust culture. That starts at the top with the owner or the CEO and the leadership team. When leaders value trust and communicate it across the entire company, trust building gets embedded into the culture and permeates the way the company behaves and does business.

The introduction of the new proprietor, Chris, and specifically his speech and the live question and answer session presented a critical trust risk point for the technology company. A critical trust risk point is anything that might undermine trust or confidence in your business.

We decide consciously and subconsciously to trust a company and its employees based on our cumulative interactions and experiences with them. Specifically, our decisions are based on how we communicate, how we behave and how we serve.

Trust has three components forming an integrated model. They include *communication* that is clear, empathetic, consistent, honest, and transparent, *behaviour* that is reliable, ethical and focused on motives to act in the customer's best interests and *service* that is sincere, predictable, reliable, empathetic, and committed to the long term.

Chris had decreased the company's Trust Equity™ at the industry conference.

A company's Trust Equity™ score is a
predictor of loyalty and future success.

Chris undermined the base of the Triangle of Trust. He violated many of the Eight Principles of Trust with his responses in the live question and answer session, saying things like "That's not a good question," "Here is a better way to look at it," "That is not our concern, I've been told it affects many in the industry, but not us," "This isn't the time or the place" or "Those that need to know that, do. Next question?"

Every single thing we do makes an impact. The ripples spread far and wide.

The Eight Principles of Trust are at the heart of how we decide to trust. In this case Chris didn't apply the principles well. To review: Chris did not behave as if he was acting in the best interests of clients (Principle #5), he did not listen or respond with empathy (Principle #1); the tone of his language was not conversational (Principle #2) or transparent (Principle #3); he surprised the audience – his behavior was not consistent with the company values (Principle #4) and he did not show commitment to the long term (Principle #8) with the response of "those that need to know know." He didn't do the right thing for the team or customers (Principle #6) nor did he deliver on the promise of being a capable leader (Principle #7).

Like many of the companies mentioned in this book, this technology company invested in the Trust Equity Accelerator program.

Their first step was to measure their Trust Equity™. Then, Chris, along with several established and up-and-coming leaders were coached. They learned the trust skill set. Knowing trust is a leadership imperative, they committed to continuous learning and improvement. Customer trust became part of the company's values, purpose, and vision. It became a beacon for everyone in the company. Together, they strove to become the most trusted in their industry.

Relationships are the lifeblood of your
business. That must be protected.

Trust is a journey, not a destination. The customer's trust in the organization is made up of the sum of the experiences they have with everyone in the company. Organizations and leaders that have high trust with their customers, suppliers, employees, and stakeholders apply the Eight Principles of Trust.

There are countless benefits to building, measuring, and protecting customer trust. My research found statistically significant, positive correlations between trust and loyalty, commitment, likelihood to recommend, satisfaction, and the intention to continue to use the company's products and services. In an atmosphere of trust, negotiations take place faster, sales cycles shorten and there are more opportunities. Loyal customers help you grow. They evangelize through their social media, their offline interactions and with friends, industry associates and family.

Building trust with customers starts inside the company, with the leader. The stronger the culture inside the company, the better equipped people are to build trust externally. With an embedded culture of trust, you'll find it easier to recruit and retain talent, while productivity and engagement soars.

When you have high customer Trust Equity™, you do not have to be continually providing and checking facts, explaining yourself and providing references and proof. Trust enables difficult and honest conversations to take place when they are needed. Trust allows organization to command a premium and to gain market share. Highly trusted companies are able to preserve and protect Trust Equity™ during difficult and challenging times.

It's everybody's responsibility to cultivate, develop and build trust. Trust is created when the customer is at the core of everything we do. And, as we've discussed, it starts at the top with the owner or the CEO and the leadership team. When trust is deemed foundational and understood, it can be managed, measured, and operationalized.

In practice, building, managing, and protecting trust requires levels of discipline and methodical action. It's about choosing to be deliberate and intentional in how we communicate, how we behave and how we serve customers.

Trust isn't just a feel-good concept—it's the bedrock of your business success. It's measurable, quantifiable, and directly linked to profitability. Your company's ability to build and maintain trust will ultimately determine your top and bottom lines. In the complex world of business, one factor stands above all others: Trust.

And the key to your long-term success? Being Trusted.

"Everyone in the organization has a part to play in the customer's decision to trust."

-Natalie Doyle Oldfield

Thank you for reading my book!

I'd welcome your feedback and would like to hear your most useful key takeaways.

Please connect with me on LinkedIn or send me an email with your feedback.

I can be reached at NOldfield@SuccessThroughTrust.com.

I'd like to hear from you.

Thank you

Natalie Doyle Oldfield

ACKNOWLEDGEMENTS

Many people have contributed to make this book possible. First, I am grateful to my clients, many of whom inspire me every single day. Thank you for sharing your customer stories, business challenges and trust issues with me. Special thanks to the graduates of the Trust Mastery, Becoming a Trusted Advisor and Trusted Leader programs – you are all extraordinary people.

I would like to take special note of my research mentor, thesis advisor and colleague Dr. Alla Kushniryk, of the Department of Communication Studies Mount Saint Vincent University. I am forever thankful to Alla. She believed in my vision to develop an evidence-based approach to a building trust framework and she supported my conclusion that Trust can be measured and quantified. Without Alla, none of this would be possible. I am grateful to Dr. Binod Sundararajan, Rowe School of Business at Dalhousie University who contributed invaluable advice and quantitative insights. My sincere thanks to the leaders and organizations who were part of the primary research. Lastly, I have a special debt of appreciation to many researchers and professionals in the field of organizational trust whose work I referenced throughout the book. I am grateful.

Special thanks to my incredible readers. I am particularly indebted to Jeff Clark, Mary Hiter, Jamie Muirhead, Derek Flynn and Macy Robison for their insights, feedback, and generosity with their time.

I feel most fortunate to have had a prize-winning journalist, editor and author, Dan Leger, applying his 'magic' and his exacting edits to this manuscript. I appreciate his guidance and diligence ensuring we have the most current data and for his wisdom.

To the many others who have helped me in one way or the other, I am grateful. The responsibility for any shortcomings or errors this book might have is entirely my own.

I'm especially grateful to my father, Arthur Doyle, who read many pages with the same enthusiasm and spark as if it was the very first and to my mother, Bonnie Doyle for putting up with our daily calls and banter. For as long as I can remember, my parents have shared their experiences and wisdom with me. To my family Heather Doyle Landry, Arthur Doyle, Bonnie Doyle Creber, and Nancy Champion, all of whom have been sources of inspiration. Bonnie, thank you for your prod to write this, we lost you too early, I'm sorry that I won't be able to share this with you.

Finally, my deepest thanks are to my children, Patrick and Courtney, and my husband Michael. All of you have enthusiastically believed in and supported this book and this research. Not only is Michael my amazing husband, he is also my business partner, my life partner, my advisor and my deepest and most enduring supporter.

Natalie Doyle Oldfield

Natalie Doyle Oldfield is the leading expert on how companies grow revenue by creating trusted relationships with customers and employees.

She is the author of *The Power of Trust: How Top Companies Build, Manage and Protect It*, and founder of Success Through Trust. Named the 'Business Trust Expert' by Economist Impact, Natalie is the creator of The Client Trust Index™, an evidence-based diagnostic that quantifies a company's Trust Equity™. Utilizing these tools along with her evidence based, proprietary Trust Building framework, Natalie has consulted with, trained, and spoken for hundreds of companies to sharpen their ability to build and maintain profitable relationships that lead to company growth by instilling her Eight Principles of Trust.

ENDNOTES

Introduction: Warning Signals, Hidden Dangers, Red Flags and Blind Spots

[1] Lin, Y. (2022). *A deeper understanding: Building trust in business partnerships*. The Economist Impact. Retrieved from https://impact.economist.com/perspectives/strategy-leadership/deeper-understanding-building-trust-business-partnerships

[2] Covey, S. M. R., & Conant, D. R. (2016, July 18). The connection between employee trust and financial performance. *Harvard Business Review*.

[3] PwC. (2024). 2024 Trust in Business Survey. Retrieved from https://www.pwc.com/us/en/library/trust-in-business-survey.html

[4] Salesforce. (2020). *State of the connected customer: 4th edition*. Salesforce. Retrieved from https://c1.sfdcstatic.com/content/dam/web/en_us/www/documents/research/salesforce-state-of-the-connected-customer-4th-ed.pdf

Principle #1 Listen Carefully, With Empathy and Compassion, Question and Involve

[5] Tamir, D. I., & Mitchell, J. P. (2012). Disclosing information about the self is intrinsically rewarding. *National Library of Medicine*. Retrieved from https://pubmed.ncbi.nlm.nih.gov/22566617/

[6] Zak, P. J. (2017). *Trust factor: The science of creating high-performance companies*. AMACOM.

[7] Zak, P.J. (2023) Immersion. *LinkedIn*.

Principle# 2 Communicate Using Clear Concrete, Conversational Language

[8] Psychology Today Staff. (n.d.). First impressions. *Psychology Today.* Retrieved from https://www.psychologytoday.com/ca/basics/first-impressions

[9] Cuddy, A. (2015). *Presence: Bringing your boldest self to your biggest challenges.* Little, Brown, & Co.

[10] Harvard Business School. (2012, November 20). First impressions: The science of meeting people. Retrieved from https://www.hbs.edu/news/Pages/item.aspx?num=284

[11] Maroño, A. (n.d.). Home. Abbie Maroño. Retrieved from https://www.abbiemarono.com

[12] Willis J, Todorov A. First impressions: making up your mind after a 100-ms exposure to a face. *Psychological Science.* 2006;17:592–8.Bar M, Neta M, Linz H. Very first impressions. *Emotion.* 2006;6(2):269–78.

[13] Todorov, A., Baron, S. G., & Oosterhof, N. N. (2008). Evaluating face trustworthiness: A model based approach. *Social Cognitive and Affective Neuroscience, 3*(2), 119–127. https://doi.org/10.1093/scan/nsn009

[14] Cited by many scholars including Walter B. Cannon (1932) The Wisdom of the Body. New York. Norton

[15] Platt, M. L., & Huettel, S. A. (2008). Risky business: The neuroeconomics of decision making under uncertainty. *Nature Neuroscience,* 11(4), 398-403.

[16] Mehrabian, A. (1971). *Silent messages: Implicit communication of emotions and attitudes.* Wadsworth Publishing.

[17] Google/Ipsos. (2024, March). The relevance factor [AU, BR, CA, FR, DE, IN, IT, JP, MX, NL, SG, KR, ES, TW, TH, U.K., U.S., VN, The Relevance Factor, n=18,003 online shoppers 18+]. Think with Google.

Principle # 3 Be Honest and Transparent

[18] Newman, D. (2015, October 13). Why customer experience is the future of marketing. *Forbes.* Retrieved from https://www.forbes.com/sites/danielnewman/2015/10/13/customer-experience-is-the-future-of-marketing/?sh=314cc358193d

[19] Lin, Y. (2022). *A deeper understanding: Building trust in business partnerships.* The Economist Impact. Retrieved from https://

impact.economist.com/perspectives/strategy-leadership/
deeper-understanding-building-trust-business-partnerships

20   Brown, B. (2021). *Atlas of the Heart: Mapping Meaningful Connection and the Language of the Human Experience*. Random House.

Principle #4 Be Consistent, Predictable and Reliable

21   Dimoka, A. (2010). What does the brain tell us about trust and distrust? Evidence from a functional neuroimaging study. *MIS Quarterly*, 34*(2), 373-396. MIS Quarterly & The Society for Information Management. Kirsch, P., Esslinger, C., Chen, Q., Mier, D., Lis, S., Siddhanti, S., Gruppe, H., Mattay, V. S., Gallhofer, B., & Meyer-Lindenberg, A. (2005). Title. *The Journal of Neuroscience*, 25(49), 11489-11493. https://doi.org/10.1523/JNEUROSCI.2556-05.2005. Uvnas-Moberg, K. (1998). Oxytocin may mediate the benefits of positive social interaction and emotions. *Psychoneuroendocrinology*, 23(8), 819-835. Elsevier Science Ltd.Van Zeeland-van der Holst, E. M., & Henseler, J. (2018). Thinking outside the box: A neuroscientific perspective on trust in B2B relationships. *IMP Journal*, 12*(1), 75-110. Emerald Publishing Limited. https://doi.org/10.1108.

22   BYJU's. (n.d.). The difference between amygdala and prefrontal cortex. Retrieved from https://byjus.com/biology/difference-between-amygdala-and-prefrontal-cortex/#:~:text=Amygdala%20are%20almond%2Dlike%20paired,frontal%20lobe%20of%20the%20brain.&text=The%20amygdala%20detects%20stress%20in%20the%20environment.

23   Epsilon. (2018). Press Release: New Epsilon research indicates 80% of consumers are more likely to make a purchase when brands offer personalized experiences. Retrieved from https://www.epsilon.com/us/about-us/pressroom/new-epsilon-research-indicates-80-of-consumers-are-more-likely-to-make-a-purchase-when-brands-offer-personalized-experiences

24   Klein, A., & Sharma, V. (2022). Consumer decision-making styles, involvement, and the intention to participate in online group buying. *Journal of Retailing and Consumer Services*, 64, 102808. https://doi.org/10.1016/j.jretconser.2021.102808

25   Lecinski, J. (2011). Winning the zero moment of truth: ZMOT. *Google*.

Principle # 5 Act in the Best Interests of Customers, Stakeholders, and the Public

[26] Kriss, P. (2014). The Value of Customer Experience, Quantified. Harvard Business Review. https://hbr.org/2014/08/the-value-of-customer-experience-quantified

Principle # 6 Do the Right Thing. If you Make a Mistake, Fix It.

[27] Gallo, A. (2014). The Value of Keeping the Right Customers. *Harvard Business Review.* Retrieved from https://hbr.org/2014/10/the-value-of-keeping-the-right-customers

[28] Pega Systems. (2020). 1-to-1 customer engagement. Retrieved from https://www.pega.com/sites/default/files/media/documents/2020-05/pega-1-to-1-customer-engagement-business-brief.pdf

[29] Badaracco, J. L. (2016). *Managing in the gray: Five timeless questions for resolving your toughest problems at work.* Harvard Business Review Press.

Principle #7 Deliver on Your Promise

[30] PR Newswire. (2022, July 1). Survey: Professional development is key to retaining talent, but people of color report less access. Retrieved from https://www.prnewswire.com/news-releases/survey-professional-development-is-key-to-retaining-talent-but-people-of-color-report-less-access-301580611.html

[31] Amabile, T. M., & Kramer, S. J. (2011). *The progress principle: Using small wins to ignite joy, engagement, and creativity at work.* Harvard Business Review Press.

[32] Harvard Business Review. (2015, March). Harvard Business School Publishing.

[33] Pfeffer, J., & Sutton, R. I. (2000). *"The Knowing-Doing Gap: How smart companies turn knowledge into action".* Harvard Business School Press.

Principle # 8 Commit to the Long Term

[34] O.C. Tanner. (2024, May 22). The business case for employee recognition. O.C. Tanner. https://www.octanner.com/white-papers/the-business-case-for-employee-recognition

35 Reilly, M. (2018, April 10). Build trust with your remote employees. Gallup. https://www.gallup.com/workplace/236222/build-trust-re-mote-employees.aspx

36 Bokman, A., Fiedler, L., Perrey, J., & Pickersgill, A. (2014, July 1). Five facts: How customer analytics boosts corporate performance. *McKinsey & Company*. https://www.mckinsey.com/capabilities/growth-marketing-and-sales/our-insights/five-facts-how-customer-analyt-ics-boosts-corporate-performance?ref=blog.42technologies.com

37 Duhigg, C. (2016, February 25). What Google learned from its quest to build the perfect team. *The New York Times Magazine*. https://www.nytimes.com/2016/02/28/magazine/what-google-learned-from-its-quest-to-build-the-perfect-team.html

38 Coyle, D. (2018). *The culture code: the secrets of highly successful groups*. Bantam Books.

Let's Continue The Conversation

My goal is that this book is not the end of the conversation about trust but the beginning. I'm interested in hearing your stories of how you and your organisations are building, managing, and protecting relationships of trust.

I encourage you to share your experiences with your friends and colleagues and to discuss how you can earn trust and loyalty of your customers to grow your business.

Unlock the Power of Trust in Your Organization – Are you and Your Team Ready?

Ready to put the principles of *Trusted* into action? Access our complimentary *Customer Readiness Checklist*. It is your fast track to identifying the gaps and opportunities on your team to implementing the trust building strategies outlined in this book. It is designed for business leaders who want to see real results fast. Visit https://www.successthroughtrust.com/ trusted for *Customer Readiness Checklist* or scan this QR code to start your journey to becoming the most Trusted in your industry today.

or visit https://www.successthroughtrust.com/

Please feel free to connect with me on LinkedIn https://www.
linkedin.com/in/nataliedoyleoldfield/